Anyone who has had the privilege [illegible] Dave Keeling would want to buy this b[illegible] to adopt even just a little bit of the ene[illegible] when creating 'aha!' – and, indeed, 'haha!' moments through playfulness and humour. Br[illegible] written with top tips and ideas that will engage even t[illegible] most challenging of audiences, *Independent Thinking on Laughter* will help you develop ways to bring energy, silliness and creativity to all learners. So open up your mind and step into these pages with all your childlike delight.

STEPHANIE DAVIES, FOUNDER AND CEO, LAUGHOLOGY

Dave Keeling takes the old saying 'Make 'em laugh, make 'em think' and transforms it into a clear, informative and enjoyable handbook that shows teachers of all age ranges how to use humour in education. *Independent Thinking on Laughter* blends an analysis of different forms of comedy into a handy DIY guide that provides a series of 'seriously funny' jokes which will make both teachers and pupils laugh out loud.

PROFESSOR MARION WYNNE-DAVIES, SCHOOL OF ENGLISH AND LANGUAGES, UNIVERSITY OF SURREY

David Keeling is the Patch Adams of education. As accountability and the pressure on schools and teachers continue to rise, *Independent Thinking on Laughter* represents a much-needed reality check on what schools, childhood and growing up is all about.

DEAN GODDARD, DEPUTY HEAD TEACHER, ST MARTIN'S SCHOOL

It seems obvious that schoolchildren like funny teachers, but perhaps it is less obvious that they might learn more when lessons are funny. In case you have ever been in any doubt about this, or simply had never thought of it before, Dave Keeling presents an extremely strong case for it in

Independent Thinking on Laughter. Your first thought, upon being convinced, may well be: 'Oh crap, I'm just not funny!' However, Dave is on hand to show you the ways in which you can harness humour for yourself, and put it to good use in your lessons.

Alongside enlightening quotations sprinkled through each chapter, Dave shares his expertise on how we can use techniques from stand-up comedy in our teaching – techniques that can be learned by those who do not necessarily have a natural talent for humour. Confidence, he explains, comes after experience, not before – a point which I have subsequently used to good effect to bolster bravery and even a little recklessness in my own students. At the end of the book he gives us a compendium of 30 exercises that can be tried right away in lessons – and what teacher doesn't love a giveaway?

This book is the perfect antidote to energy-sapping staffroom cynics – an optimistic and joyful shot in the arm for anyone who feels their enthusiasm for teaching might be slipping. Laugh off those directives and specification changes, and give your teaching a humour injection.

JANE WERRY, DIRECTOR OF MUSIC/ LEAD TEACHER, HAYES SCHOOL

A delightful book that concisely brings together some of the key ideas and facts about the positive impact of laughter in order to make the case for the use of humour in the educational setting.

DR KATHARINE LOW, SENIOR LECTURER, COMMUNITY PERFORMANCE AND APPLIED THEATRE, ROYAL CENTRAL SCHOOL OF SPEECH AND DRAMA

INDEPENDENT
THINKING
ON ...

LAUGHTER

Dave Keeling

USING HUMOUR AS A TOOL TO ENGAGE
AND MOTIVATE ALL LEARNERS

independent
thinking press

First published by

Independent Thinking Press
Crown Buildings, Bancyfelin, Carmarthen, Wales, SA33 5ND, UK
www.independentthinkingpress.com

and

Independent Thinking Press
PO Box 2223, Williston, VT 05495, USA
www.crownhousepublishing.com

Independent Thinking Press is an imprint of
Crown House Publishing Ltd.

This edition first published 2020.

Orignally published as *The Little Book of Laughter* ISBN: 978-178135008-9

Edited by Ian Gilbert.

The Independent Thinking On ... series is typeset in Azote, Buckwheat TC Sans, Cormorant Garamond and Montserrat.

The Independent Thinking On ... series cover style was designed by Tania Willis www.taniawillis.com.

British Library Cataloguing-in-Publication Data
A catalogue entry for this book is available from the British Library.

Print ISBN 978-178135341-7
Mobi ISBN 978-178135344-8
ePub ISBN 978-178135345-5
ePDF ISBN 978-178135346-2

LCCN 2019951749

Printed and bound in the UK by
Gomer Press, Llandysul, Ceredigion

For my wife, Kate, who laughs with me every day.

FOREWORD

Since establishing Independent Thinking in 1994, we have worked hard to share with educators around the world our belief that there is always another way. The Independent Thinking On ... series of books is an extension of that work, giving a space for great educators to use their words and share great practice across a number of critical and relevant areas of education.

Independent Thinking on Laughter is the very embodiment of the phrase we have used for quite some time: that education is far too important to be taken seriously. While 'having a laugh' might seem like the last thing children should – or teachers could – be doing in our classrooms currently, the evidence for cracking a smile is compelling. Whether it's developing better relationships, improving behaviour, raising academic achievement or creating a school where everyone's health and well-being is that bit better, laughter is the silver bullet you are looking for. The neuroscience backs this up, as does the experience of simply being in a classroom in which everyone is genuinely enjoying themselves.

And when it comes to ensuring that everyone in the room is enjoying themselves, there are few better at achieving this than stand-up comic and Independent Thinking Associate Dave Keeling. Drawing on many years' experience of standing in front of – and quickly winning over – a hostile crowd, whether that's a hall full of Year 10s or a hen party on a night out, Dave shows teachers everywhere the tricks of the trade that will ensure that you bring energy, enjoyment and laughter to each and every lesson in a way that will benefit everyone.

We are constantly raising the stakes for young people in the education system and piling on the pressure for them to succeed. Going to school is a serious business these days, but – as Dave Keeling proves in this entertaining book – that doesn't mean to say that learning is no laughing matter.

After all, smile and the world smiles with you, *** and you *** alone.[1]

IAN GILBERT
BRIGHTON

1 Insert your own joke here.

ACKNOWLEDGEMENTS

I would like to thank:

Everyone at Crown House Publishing for their support and for allowing me the freedom to follow my passions and share them with others. Your efforts on my behalf are always greatly appreciated.

Ian Gilbert for his wit, wisdom and one-liners that have helped me hugely in the creation of this comical compendium (anything to do with cats is his!).

To anyone who has ever sniggered, giggled, howled or cried with laughter as a result of something I have said or done. It's all your fault – I wouldn't do it if you didn't laugh. You are the very reason that, as a youngster, I never listened to my mum whenever she said, 'Stop showing off.' Please keep egging me on.

And finally, I would like to thank everyone and anyone who has, over the period of my life, done or said anything that has made me laugh my head off! You have all made me very, very happy.

CHEERS

CONTENTS

FIRST THOUGHTS

> *Something which has never occurred since time immemorial: a young woman did not fart in her husband's lap.*

Now this Sumerian one-liner dating back to 1900 BC might not be the best gag ever, but it is the oldest. Or at least the oldest on record. Cavemen probably had their own version in a *Blazing Saddles* meets *One Million Years BC* sort of way. Laughter, relationships and bodily functions are clearly a part of what makes us human and they certainly form a core part of classroom life, as anyone with a large bottom set will tell you (pun intended).

This little book of mirth seeks to take you on a brief but enlightening journey into exactly what laughter is and what part the use of humour can play in enhancing and galvanising the learning experience for all concerned.

Like Ant and Dec, there are two parts to this book: the first is short, witty and sets the scene; the second is a little bit shorter and funnier. In the first section, I have included all the information and handy hints I could muster from my tour of the world of humour and comedy, ideas that I believe will steadfastly aid and assist teachers in their bid to bring a little more light relief to the classroom. Along the way, I will strive to demystify the art and science of laughter and explore how to seek out and create moments where laughter can occur to make things in the classroom better all round.

The second section consists of a veritable smorgasbord of exercises and activities for use with learners in your classroom – activities proven to create humour, generate laughter, enhance learning and make you look great. Your mission, if you choose to accept it, is to take these ideas and exercises and adopt, adapt, enjoy, explore and generally mess about with them to your heart's content.

Of course, there's more than one way to cook an egg (as my B in GCSE home economics proudly signifies), and I am not in the least suggesting these ideas are the only way to get 'em rolling in the aisles. But like a chicken and an egg, or an egg and a chicken (I never know which comes first), they're a start.

It is also worth mentioning that all the ideas, thoughts, feelings, activities, hints and suggestions in this book have come together through years of plugging away in front of audiences of students, parents, teachers, businesses and the general public. Audiences as big as a thousand and as little as three. Audiences that have ranged the full gamut from warm, welcoming, funny, excited, inspiring and up for it (you'd be surprised) to cold, hostile, indifferent, arrogant, disaffected and downright angry. As one man wrote on his feedback sheet: 'Dave Keeling has the sort of face I would never tire of slapping' (there are easier ways to flirt!).

My hope is that this book will, in some small way, give you permission to have as much fun as possible in your classroom and will, en route, inform, empower and entertain in equal measure. After all, having a laugh should be in your job description because, let's face it, if you don't love what you do, why should the kids? And let me reassure you too. Some people believe that you are either funny or you are not. I disagree. Later on in this book, I'll give away some of the secrets that comedians use to create laughter. But, for now, take heart from the fact that everyone can be funny and use humour to enhance the way they work. Trust me, I'm ginger!

So, sit back on your whoopee cushion of learning, rub grease on your funny bone, plaster an intrigued smile across your face and imagine everyone around you is naked, as I endeavour to explain what this funny business is all about.

My act is very educational. I heard a man leaving the other night saying, 'Well, that taught me a lesson.'

KEN DODD

PART I
THE WORLD OF HUMOUR AND COMEDY

Education: A technique employed to open minds so that they may go from cocksure ignorance to thoughtful uncertainty.

CHAPTER 1

FUNNY BUSINESS IS A RISKY BUSINESS

Don't worry, don't be afraid, because this is just a ride.

BILL HICKS

Just before we crack on, a quick word of warning. This may only be a little book but taking on board the ideas and the philosophies within it will demand some big risks. Yet, as John Vorhaus states in his opus, *The Comic Toolbox*: 'What we don't always have is the will to risk, and the will to risk is really the will to fail. Behind all bogus thinking is the biggest bogus thought of all: If I fail I die.'[1]

So, there you have it. No one was harmed in the making of this book and no one will be harmed while reading it. You will not die as a result of implementing the ideas contained herein and all will be well. Cross my heart and hope to die (me, not you). All I ask is that in order to get the black-and-white pages of this book up and running, you allow yourself to indulge in the art of play.

Never trust a man who, when left alone in a room with a tea cosy, doesn't try it on.

BILLY CONNOLLY

1 J. Vorhaus, *The Comic Toolbox: How to Be Funny Even if You're Not* (Beverly Hills, CA: Silman-James Press, 1994), pp. 9, 11.

Play is at the heart of human development. It shapes our thinking, relationships, imagination and emotional regulation. Play is a practical endeavour and is born out of an inherent need for exploration. Play signals, such as eye contact, touch, laughter and smiling, are the basis of our very first communicative interactions with the world. Laughter and humour are a major factor in social play and help to forge friendships and create a sense of equality. Learning should therefore be a collaborative enterprise, a mutual exchange of knowledge, thoughts and ideas. Not a 'them and us' but simply a single, happy 'us'. All in it together, learning well and having a laugh as we go.

Simply answer 'yes' to the following statements and I'll let you carry on reading this book, safe in the knowledge that the universe, or at the very least your classroom, will be a better place as a result.

I am funny.

I am a risk taker.

I am open to all ideas.

I am what I am.

I am the walrus, goo goo g'joob.

Clearly, embracing risk isn't without its, er, risks and, like anything in life, it is worth remembering these four golden nuggets of wisdom when attempting something new:

1 What do you want? If you know what you want you are much more likely to get it.

2 Think of the positives. There must always be something in it for you. Remind yourself why you are doing what you are doing and what those benefits will look like.

3 Recognise the obstacles. Be as sure as you can about what may get in the way to prevent you from moving

forward. If you have an idea of what you might face you'll be better prepared to navigate a way around it. Even if it's a blank map with 'Here be monsters' on it, it's better than nothing (unless you have a sat nav, in which case you'll most probably end up lying in a ditch hearing the haunting and repetitive refrain of 'You've reached your destination').

4 Have the confidence to find out. Mr Micawber, in David Copperfield, says 'Procrastination is the thief of time', and it will also take all your money and your energy and leave you with nothing but the corduroy jacket you stand up in, unless you actually act upon what you have taken the effort and expense to read in this book. So, in the words of Hedley Lamarr in *Blazing Saddles*, 'Go do that voodoo that you do so well.'[2]

'Confidence is half the battle,' they say. I shouldn't imagine that's official military advice ... 'Sorry, the guns have jammed and we've lost all our armour, but we still have positive body language; that ought to see us through some desert combat.'

MILES JUPP

2 If you haven't seen the film *Blazing Saddles* then you should; it is very, very funny.

CHAPTER 2

WHAT A SENSE OF HUMOUR IS AND HOW TO DEFINE IT

Men will confess to treason, murder, arson, false teeth, or a wig. How many of them will own up to a lack of humour?

FRANK MOORE COLBY

It has been argued that a sense of humour is, perhaps, the most important quality any person can possess. Let's face it, would you admit to not having one? But what exactly is it and how do you define it?

Well, starting with the obvious, as most humour does, the *Collins Concise Dictionary* suggests humour is 'the quality of being fun' and 'a state of mind'. (I tried looking in *Webster's American English Dictionary* but they couldn't even spell it properly.) A less obvious place to look for a definition is the 17th century, but this is where we find the English philosopher Thomas Hobbes referring to humour in the delightful phrase, a 'sudden Glory'. In other words, he was describing that moment when a funny connection is made between things or people and explodes into a little ejaculation of joy (stop it!), or as one epigram goes: 'Laughter is an orgasm triggered by the intercourse of sense and nonsense.' (Every day's a learning day.)

Have a think about the last 'sudden Glory' you enjoyed (behave) and the effect that it had on you and those around you. Where do your lesson plans, your curriculum or your whole-school ethos make space for such sudden glories?

Humour and laughter are indeed bedfellows but they are, in fact, very different beings. Like Morecambe and Wise. So, while humour is something we can learn, hence this book, is laughter the same? The short answer is 'no'. Although, that said, the long answer is also 'no'.

Humour is a way of seeing the world, a way of processing information, a philosophy, an attitude, a lifestyle choice, a gift and a burden all at the same time. With a sense of humour, no matter what happens, you will always see the funny side. Useful at funerals. The trouble is, with a sense of humour, you always see the funny side. Dangerous at funerals. That said, once we know what humour really is, it opens up a whole world of possibility when it comes to engaging with others in a learning context. Although humour is very much an inner process, it is something that can be projected to others through visual cues, verbal communication, body language and other everyday means.

Comedians use humour as a way to communicate their worldview to an audience in a fun and entertaining way. When this is done with great skill, confidence, verbal dexterity and wit, we, the audience, get the benefit of the comedian's humour, sharing with them, albeit briefly, the manner in which they see the world, looking at life through the lens of someone with a keen sense of the ridiculous in the serious. And, on a good day, we show our appreciation by not throwing things and, on a very good day, through the shared medium of laughter.

> *I know I've got a degree. Why does that mean I have to spend my life with intellectuals? I've got a lifesaving certificate but I don't spend my evenings diving for a rubber brick with my pyjamas on.*
>
> VICTORIA WOOD

So, it is clear that humour is an internal, cognitive processing tool, whereas laughter is the outer manifestation of the mirth, amusement and joy we are experiencing, the pay-off for the humour, the involuntary communicative act that lets someone know they have succeeded in their quest for funny, even if that was involuntary in a 'man slips on banana skin' way (I'm still waiting to witness this event).

It is important to observe, too, that while humour is something one person can do on their own at night if there's nothing on the goggle box, laughter is a process by which we can satisfy our desire to connect with others and express how we are feeling. Humour is social self-esteem. It is an intrinsic part of the human condition. Coming up with a joke while out with friends is socially permitted. Laughing at it so hard that you pee yourself, less so.

In their study of laughter, gelotologists[1] Matthew Gervais and David Sloan Wilson state that laughter in primates first evolved from play panting some seven million years ago. It wasn't until between two and four million years ago that we developed the capacity to control our 'facial motor systems' and utilise them to communicate our feelings towards others and manage social situations: 'Humans can now voluntarily access the laughter program and utilize it for their own ends, including smoothing conversational

1 From the Greek *gelotos* meaning laughter - not the Italian *gelato* meaning ice cream.

interaction, appeasing others, inducing favourable stances in them, or downright laughing at people that are not liked.'[2]

So, there you have it. We probably laughed at farty jokes before we evolved the language to talk about mothers-in-law.[3]

> *Your mother has spent 44 years trying to change me and now she says I'm not the man she married.*
>
> **MY DAD**

And while I am on the subject of gasbagging, here are the top eight reasons as to why humour is essential as a communication tool in learning:

1 Keeps students' attention.

2 Emphasises key points so they stand out, allowing for better retention.

3 Can make facts and data easier to digest.

4 Can help regain control more effectively after a disturbance.

5 Can relax an audience, creating a better sense of unity.

6 Keeps relationships exciting, fresh, sparky, fun and healthy.

7 Enriches daily interactions.

---

2 M. Gervais and D. S. Wilson, The Evolutions and Functions of Laughter and Humor: A Synthetic Approach, *Quarterly Review of Biology* 80(4) (2005): 395–430 at 418.

3 Other in-laws are also available for ridicule.

8 Can be used as a tool to build resilience. Laughing about setbacks helps us to take them in our stride, distance ourselves from them personally and bounce back from disappointment much quicker.

Comedy is a group activity, a verbal orgy.

CHRIS ROCK

For humour to elicit laughter, you, the individual, have to be in a good mood (c'mon, it won't kill you) and this mood needs to permeate to those around you. They need to feel this energy coming from you in order to establish the right environment for humour and laughter to take place. Your attitude will set the tone that others can follow. So, knowing what puts you in 'good humour' to start with is a great advantage to setting you on the road to creating a classroom that is playful, fun and full of innovative learning.

So, how does one go about achieving good humour?

1 **How you view the world.**

Whether you are a glass half-empty sort of person (i.e. negative) or a 'you can't polish a turd but you can roll it in glitter' type of person (i.e. always looking for the positive).[4]

2 **How you feel.**

The frame of mind you are in is heavily influenced by what is happening in your personal/professional life, what you are doing at any given time and how you deal with it.

4 Or, as Oscar Wilde so succinctly put it, 'Some people create happiness wherever they go; others whenever they go.'

3 **How you choose to act and respond to the world around you.**

There is an area of the brain called the supplementary motor which can associate movement with positive feelings. This means that even the suggestion of a particular movement can bring about the feeling of well-being.

When the mouth is open for laughter, you can pop in some food for thought.

ANONYMOUS

This is where it gets interesting and where you can think about changing your mood and creating good humour, for you and others. A simple example of this is that when we feel happy we start to smile, but if we smile we also start to feel happy.

Try it now. Wherever you are, whatever you're doing, just stop, and smile.

Feel different? Good.

It is imperative that you are aware of the behaviours you display when you're in 'good humour'. The more familiar you are with these, the easier it will be to repeat these behaviours and recreate your good mood at will. This, in turn, will impact on the mood of the people around you in a positive way. In order to help you recognise what Stephanie Davies, author of *Laughology: Improve Your Life with the Science of Laughter*, calls your 'good humour ingredients'[5] you will need to pay particular attention to the following:

5 S. Davies, *Laughology: Improve Your Life with the Science of Laughter* (Carmarthen: Crown House Publishing, 2013), p. 88.

- Your body language.
- Your facial expressions.
- Your voice – including its tone, pitch and pace.
- The types of words you use.

So, next time you're in a good mood (it will happen, trust me) think about how you use your body. Do you gesticulate more? Do you lean forward to draw other people in to you? Are you relaxed? Does your voice go an octave higher? Do your eyes sparkle? What happens to your face? What language do you use? Is it more colourful? More descriptive? A bit blue (your language, not your face)? Do you talk quicker? Do you laugh more? Do you breathe more quickly?

By understanding these traits and habits, and getting into the habit of repeating them, you will find that you have instant access to 'good humour' and a positive frame of mind whenever you want it – and so will be more able to make better choices for yourself, while simultaneously enhancing your mood.

What's more, by changing your mood you can start to change the disposition of those around you. And, as a teacher, that's one of the best skills we can have – to be able to get our learners into a better state of mind for learning simply by being in our presence.

> *Even if there is nothing to laugh about, laugh on credit.*
>
> **ANONYMOUS**

While this process, which is known as 'emotional contagion', is a very subtle way of influencing those around you, there are also some less subtle but equally effective ways of creating 'good humour' across the whole class. Here are three of my favourites:

1 Get the class moving. If students are sitting still for too long they will become slouched, apathetic and unfocused in body as well as mind. Simply get them to stand up and pull a funny face, play a game or move about in some way. 'Fartlek' your sessions as much as possible.[6] Get their minds thinking and their bodies moving in positive ways to back up the content of the lesson and help augment the learning that is taking place. Put a group of people through a quick, common experience, such as a game, and it has the simple but profound effect of galvanising the group due to the new, shared adventure ('Do you remember when we ...?').

2 Invest in a service bell, buzzer or sound cue of some sort. Train your learners, Pavlov dog-style,[7] that when they hear it they have to sit up, lean forward and imagine that what you are about to tell them is the most interesting thing they have ever heard. Encouraging your learners to massively exaggerate their response to new learning by mock shock, laughter, horror or excitement can greatly enhance their ability to enjoy the new knowledge and aid their recall. If your students don't arrive in 'good humour' then take the power back by using the technique above and instruct/trick them into it.

3 Get mischievously creative. Think about ways to be naughty and subvert the learning. You could show them a comedy clip from YouTube, play them a funny song, show them an amusing picture, tell them a

6 *Fartlek* is Swedish for 'speed-play', that is to say interval training.

7 A classical conditioning system, not a euphemism.

story, get them to dance – absolutely anything that will encourage play and laughter.

Laughter is the shortest distance between two people.

VICTOR BORGE

Our ability to change our moods as a result of a change to our actions is due to the fact that we are what has been called 'psychophysical beings'. In other words, our minds affect our bodies and our bodies affect our minds. So, the fastest way to change your mind is to change the way you behave and vice versa. Furthermore, our ability to shift our state and impact the mood of those around us gives us a much greater degree of control when it comes to teaching or, indeed, engaging with a group on any level. Look at it like this: being conscious of our actions and behaviours is one thing; being conscious of our reactions to the world and how that impacts on our mood is a whole new ball game, especially when so much of it is taking place at a subconscious level.

In a neurological nutshell, our right brain is constantly scanning the world around us for things of interest (for example, things we can eat or things that eat us). When something enters our radar that is worthy of further notice, it is 'squirted' (in the descriptive words of Dr Andrew Curran, our resident paediatric neurologist at Independent Thinking) over to our left brain, which starts to analyse it and link it with other parts of our brain associated with feelings, emotions and memory. Although it might seem self-evident, we tend to forget the fact that the 'thing' itself does not exist in our head. What does, if you can call it *exist*, is a 3D representation of that outer thing in our mind's eye. It only exists because we create what is called an 'internal representation' of it. We then give this a name and an emotional response, which then informs our behaviour.

So, for instance, we see a tree worthy of note. We create a 3D representation of the tree in our mind's eye. We then give it a name – 'Tree'. We then have an emotional response such as 'I love trees' or 'Ooh, look, firewood!' This response then has an impact on our behaviour – 'I want to hug the tree' or 'Where's my axe?'

So now that you know exactly how our brains work (nothing to it really), try this little thought experiment. Imagine a colleague coming into your classroom to tell you that there is either (a) a cat, (b) a cake, (c) a parent, (d) a journalist, (e) a psychiatrist or (f) an Ofsted inspector waiting in reception for you. Your behaviour would change as a result of your emotional response to each one and, as Shakespeare would say in the bath, there's the rub. When you are seeking to take control of your moods, and use them in a positive way to enhance learning, you must be aware of your actions and reactions and seek to be in control of them, and not the other way round. It takes practice but it can be done. As the Greek philosopher Epictetus once said, 'It's not what happens to you, but how you react to it that matters.' The belief here being that you only have influence over two things in life: what you think and what you do. Everything else is out of your control. So what are you thinking and how are you thinking (is it helpful or hindering?), and what are you doing to back it up?

If all you can control is your thoughts, then you are well on the way to influencing everyone around you for the better. By maintaining your good humour, you are in a position to maintain theirs and everyone will win. With such control, you can build effective working relationships with students, grab their attention, lure them into learning what you want them to learn, bring them back to task at will, and put material over in a variety of interesting and enjoyable ways, which will mean that the behaviour within a group takes care of itself and you are guaranteed to elicit a much more favourable response to the phrase, 'In today's lesson we will be ...'

But don't take my word for it. Give it a go and set yourself a task. Next time you are in a lesson and you aren't quite getting the response you want, do something different but humorous to elicit a laugh and effect a change of state in both yourself and the class. This could be as simple as a quick game (see Chapter 8) to move them about, telling a joke, asking a challenging question or even just suggesting that they have a quick cuddle with the person next to them. See how many ways you can quickly change the mood of a room (without harming any cats, obviously).

> *We spend the first twelve months of our children's lives teaching them to walk and talk, and the next twelve years telling them to sit down and shut up.*
>
> PHYLLIS DILLER

CHAPTER 3

HUMOUR, CURIOSITY AND PLAYFULNESS – BEING 7 ALL OVER AGAIN

Growing old is compulsory, growing up is optional.

BOB MONKHOUSE

A statistic that is often bandied around regarding laughter states that children laugh up to 300 times a day whereas adults laugh only around 17 times a day. That said, I've seen plenty of adults who never laugh, although that might just be the nature of the INSET I was doing at the time.

What is it that these kids know that we don't? Why do they get to have all the fun while we adults slave away day after day without so much as a whiff of a Jelly Baby, star of the week certificate or times-table badge for our troubles?

I firmly believe that there is much to be gleaned from copying a child's approach to life, laughter and learning, and it starts with that wonderful little word – curiosity.

Curiosity is the natural inclination to question, challenge and make sense of the world around us. This wonderful quality is inherent in every youngster and comes from a deep-seated desire to understand and be understood. In the words of the 20th-century philosopher Wittgenstein: 'Humour is not a mood but a way of looking at the world.'

For me, humour is quite simply what you get when you are curious about the world around you in a playful way. Like a 7-year-old. Or me with a firework at parents' evening.

But let me break down that explanation further. Curiosity is one thing. It brings out the philosopher in us, and the scientist. The word 'curiosity' has the same Latin root as the word 'curator' and it means to look after, to care for, to take care of. But curiosity alone does not produce humour. The manner in which we are curious is critical, too, and it is vital that we approach this curiosity in a playful way. Like a child.

> *I won't say I was a slow developer, but our teacher was quite pleased to have someone her own age in the class to talk to.*
>
> **CHARLES 'CHIC' MURRAY**

A child's love of nonsense, their desire to engage and explore regardless of who's watching, their lack of self-editing, their propensity for mischief, their capacity for just being in the moment wherever that moment may take them, all of this turns little human beings into wonderfully natural humour monkeys. And I love a humour monkey.

So, when was the last time you were genuinely curious about something? If you're having trouble answering this question, then think about when was the last time you found out something completely new about your partner? Or your kids? Or your best friend? When did you last discover something you never knew before about the place where you live? Where you work? About the subject you teach? And while I have you on my couch, when were you last genuinely and unapologetically playful? When was the last time you got up to some sort of recalcitrant behaviour? When did you last get naughty in your job? And if you've never got naughty in your job, if you were to get naughty in your job, what would you do for your first time?

Curiosity can prepare the ground for humour, and, in my experience, one of the best and most effective ways to pique a group's curiosity – and from there change their mood and open them up to the wonderful world of learning for the better – is to do, show or say something that no one expects. Something that will turn their expectations upside down.

Here is a selection from the shelves of my own curiosity shop:

- Have a strange object on your desk.
- Make an intentional mistake.
- Play music they may never have heard before.
- Wear a costume as they come into the room.
- Arrange the room in a different layout (this will pique their curiosity and immediately get them asking questions).
- Have a special guest in the classroom.
- Use food of any description and in any manner.
- Stand on your desk (health and safety decrees you must have a ladder and an ambulance on standby for this one).
- Play with a £50 note (if you haven't got one, ask someone in reprographics to print you one up – you know they'll know what to do!).
- Arrive slightly late, make a big entrance and use a word that no one has ever heard of.

Try any of the above – or come up with your own – and prepare to be amazed at how inundated you will be with more inquisitive questions than you can shake a stick at. In fact, shaking a stick at them – there's another one.

In his book *Taking Laughter Seriously*, doctor of philosophy and founder of the International Society for Humor Studies John Morreall[1] explains that the first principle of comedy is for the comedian to engage the interest of those he wants to amuse by enabling the audience 'to feel familiar with him and interested in what he's saying, so that he can set them up for the mental shifts of his humour'.[2] In other words, get 'em curious about what is about to happen so you can reel them in and play around with their presumptions. Morreall's second principle builds off this first technique. He says: 'Humour involves a disturbance of our ordinary patterns of thought and expectation, a jolt to our picture of reality ... Humour works only by contrast with ordinary patterns of reality.'[3]

Another way of looking at this is what the writer Arthur Koestler calls 'bisociation' – the humour that is to be found at the point where two previously unrelated ideas converge unexpectedly, where the day-to-day journey we thought we were on becomes interrupted by a judge with a grudge and little bit of fudge and a wary canary with a belly full of balls.[4]

So, turning your students' expectations and assumptions upside down early on creates an air of excitement and a frisson of anticipation. That said, I'm not suggesting at this point that we should make everything we do funny. Our

1 Not to be confused with Professor Yaffle Chucklebutty, Operatic Tenor and Sausage Knotter, as Ken Dodd was once known.

2 J. Morreall, *Taking Laughter Seriously* (Albany, NY: State University of New York Press, 1983), p. 83.

3 Ibid.

4 Blame Vic Reeves for that one.

'audience' will soon become bored with the familiarity of this pattern of unfamiliarity and when they are constantly expecting the unexpected you will lose the 'jolt' you were looking for.

> *Apparently, one in five people in the world are Chinese. And there are five people in my family, so it must be one of them. It's either my mum or my dad. Or my older brother, Colin. Or my younger brother, Ho-Chan-Chu. But I think it's Colin.*
>
> **TIM VINE**

As Morreall says, describing his third principle of what makes for good humour, there is a 'necessity of originality and freshness': 'If the audience is to experience a mental shift, they must be caught off guard with something they cannot smoothly assimilate.'[5]

If we take all of the above into account, what it tells us is that it is imperative we continue to play around as much as we can with the structures and strictures that come with modern-day teaching and learning. If we constantly seek to defy expectations and present content that is thoughtful, challenging, exciting *and* unexpected, we will not only enable our students to get more out of their time in our classrooms but also create a classroom culture that is filled with enjoyment and chock full of possibility. In doing so, we help to ensure the brains of our young learners are constantly fired, fried and stimulated by the events within the classroom (more of which in Chapter 4).

Now, for those of you doing the 'That's all well and good but what about Ofsted?' routine that I have heard so often, then please feel free to check your copies of Ofsted's *Education*

5 Morreall, *Taking Laughter Seriously*, p. 83.

Inspection Handbook or *Framework for School Inspection*. C'mon, you know you've got copies somewhere.

These publications continue to highlight the important role that well-being and relationships play in learning and in the development of young people:

- *the provider has high expectations for learners' behaviour and conduct*
- *learners' attitudes to their education or training are positive.*
- *relationships among learners and staff reflect a positive and respectful culture.*
- *the provider prepares learners for life in modern Britain by:*
    - *equipping them to be responsible, respectful, active citizens who contribute positively to society*[6]

And what better than having a laugh in the classroom to achieve practically all of these things. If it's good enough for Ofsted ...

> *My problems all started with my early education. I went to a school for mentally disturbed teachers.*
>
> **WOODY ALLEN**

But what about life beyond the classroom? If we teach children that being emotionally engaged through humour is an effective way of bringing out their best, what will happen to them when they meet the big bad world of work? Well, according to Pulitzer Prize winning author and journalist Thomas L. Friedman, the future is not just in the

6 Ofsted, *The Education Inspection Framework*. Ref: 190015 (2019). Available at: https://assets.publishing.service.gov.uk/government/uploads/system/uploads/attachment_data/file/801429/Education_inspection_framework.pdf.

hands of those with high levels of intelligence but those with outstanding levels of passion and curiosity too. As he wrote in a 2013 article for the *New York Times*: 'The winners won't just be those with more I.Q. It will also be those with more P.Q. (passion quotient) and C.Q. (curiosity quotient) to leverage all the new digital tools to not just find a job, but to invent one or reinvent one, and to not just learn but to relearn for a lifetime.'

I don't know about you, but I would rather work with someone who was curious and passionate about what they were doing rather than someone who was just qualified. A curious and passionate learner will be intrinsically motivated to learn their whole life long. They won't just do the bare minimum to get by. In the classroom, these are the children who are smart enough to tell you what they think you want to hear but never go beyond that and learn for themselves. When you were at school, how many times did you try to guess what was inside your teacher's head, in the hope that you could then say it quickly and be left alone? That's not learning, folks – that's survival, and it's a very different thing. We don't want our children to survive their education; surely we want them to engage with it and be engaged by it.

> *Trying to give my kids an education in Los Angeles is a nightmare with the guns, the gangs, the drugs – and I'm home schooling them.*
>
> **DAVID FELDMAN**

If we can encourage and empower our young people to continue to be naturally inquisitive, to learn and to love learning and to do so *with heart*, then that has to be a good thing. And humour – yes, having a laugh as they learn – is your shortcut to making that happen.

All of which brings me neatly to neoteny. There, I've said it! Juvenilisation! There I go again. Pedomorphism! Oops, that one just slipped out. Neoteny (otherwise known as juvenilisation or pedomorphism) is not only a lovely word, it is also the name given to the study of juvenile traits in adults. Desmond Morris, famous zoologist and author of *The Naked Ape*, attributes the process of neoteny to the huge evolutionary step that brought about a massive shift in human brainpower and allowed man to neurologically dominate the planet. Or as my dad eloquently once said of me, 'If he had a brain he'd be dangerous.'

In fact, it was Bruce Charlton, Reader in Evolutionary Psychiatry at Newcastle University, who first introduced the phrase 'psychological neoteny' to the waiting world of serious grown-ups. He explains that: 'We are expected to adapt to change throughout our lives, both in our personal relationships and in our careers. The ability to retain youthful qualities, now often seen as folly, may someday be recognized as a prized trait.' This is because, he goes on to say (in a decidedly un-neotenous manner) in his paper 'The Rise of the Boy-Genius: Psychological Neoteny, Science and Modern Life':

> *The mid-twentieth century saw the rise of the boy-genius, probably because a personality type characterized by prolonged youthfulness is advantageous both in science and modern life generally. ... A child-like flexibility of attitudes, behaviours and knowledge is probably adaptive in modern society because people need repeatedly to change jobs, learn new skills, move to new places and make new friends.*
>
> *The modern exemplary geriatric should continue to compete for high status, remain actively interested in love and sex,*

> *show themselves adaptive to change and continually seek new experiences and challenges.*[7]

This is not only a welcome shot in the arm for my grandad (who will need a shot in the arm to fulfil his part of the bargain) but also further proof that, as a species, we are the most neotenous, youthful, flexible, plastic and playful there is, all of which makes us the most adaptable. And by adaptable I mean able to learn new things. Perfect for school then! So, developing a more open, playful, childlike side to yourself can vastly increase your ability to think in a more positive and imaginative way, to adapt, to learn and to survive.

Richard Branson is a good example of a neotenous grown-up who can readily call upon his inner 7-year-old. His job basically consists of playing with planes, trains, hot air balloons, boats, desert islands, other people's money. This is a man whose imagination has taken him from transatlantic to intergalactic. A man who takes what he does very seriously but knows when to seriously play. As he says in his book, *Screw It, Let's Do It*: 'Fun refreshes us. I often ask myself, is my work fun and does it make me happy? I believe the answer to that is more important than fame or fortune. If something stops being fun, I ask why? If I can't fix it, I stop doing it.'[8] He goes on to say: 'Think young and by that, I don't mean you have to be young or you're over the hill at thirty. People who stop thinking and feeling young tend to be rigid in their approach to life and that's not what creativity, growth and personal development is all about.'[9]

---

7 B. G. Charlton, The Rise of the Boy-Genius: Psychological Neoteny, Science and Modern Life, *Medical Hypotheses* 67(4) (2006): 679–681. Available at: http://www.hedweb.com/bgcharlton/ed-boygenius.html.

8 R. Branson, *Screw It, Let's Do It: Lessons in Life* (London: Virgin Books/Ebury, 2006), pp. 32–33.

9 Branson, *Screw It, Let's Do It*, pp. 200–201.

Are you thinking young? How readily can you access your inner 7-year-old? Do you know how to tap into a more playful, imaginative and flexible state? If you do, then the world of the 21st century is whatever mollusc you want it to be because now, more than ever, the world needs people who possess the qualities of versatility, creativity, innovation and playfulness.

> *A man loses his dog, so he puts an ad in the newspaper and it reads, 'Here boy!'*
>
> **SPIKE MILLIGAN**

CHAPTER 4

THE SCIENCEY BIT – IT'S BRAIN JIM, BUT NOT AS WE KNOW IT

How is 'education' supposed to make me smarter? Besides, every time I learn something new, it pushes some old stuff out of my brain. Remember when I took that home wine-making course and I forgot how to drive?

HOMER SIMPSON

Even a quick trawl through the many books and articles on the health-bestowing benefits of laughter would take you a while, as I have found to my cost. So, let me save you the time and effort by giving you the edited highlights.

Laughter ...

1 Releases endorphins. (Or, if you want to sound even more cleverer, endogenous opioid peptides. Yes, 'opioid'. You know what that means.) These are naturally occurring neurochemicals that produce a feeling of well-being and are released during the consumption of spicy foods, exercise, excitement, pain, love and orgasm. But enough of my weekend. That's one helluva chemical.

2 Boosts the immune system. It increases the number of antibody-producing cells and enhances the effectiveness of T-cells (a type of white blood cell that

helps to mediate K-cells or killer cells), leading to a stronger immune system all round.

3 Decreases stress hormones such as cortisol. Cortisol is released by the adrenal glands into the bloodstream – and high levels of it in the blood can lead to high blood pressure, lowered immunity, blood sugar imbalance and impaired cognitive performance. High levels of cortisol as a child set our 'stress thermostat' to high as an adult, so the more we can mediate high levels in children, the better in the long run. Although some children aren't so much victims of stress as carriers.

4 Relaxes the whole body. As well as enhancing our mood, having a good laugh can do wonders for the relief of ` tension and stress. Remember this saying: 'Sometimes I laugh so hard tears run down my leg.'

5 Protects the heart. Laughter can increase blood flow and improve the function of the blood vessels. The knock-on effect is a healthy heart and a reduction in cardiovascular problems. At this juncture, a lesser comic would insert a joke about infarctions but no, not me, I shall rise above it ...

6 Makes you more attractive (I might have made this up but, hey ho, fingers crossed).

7 Means you live longer. Yep, a giggle a day keeps death away, whereas if you spend your days walking around with a face like a smacked backside there is every possibility that you may check out from this mortal realm much earlier than someone who is more optimistic, expects good things to happen and seeks out positive experiences.

8 Helps with 'sticky' learning. When you are emotionally connected to a particular piece of learning, that

information has a better chance of sticking. The emotional part of our brain and the long-term memory part of our brain are one and the same (the limbic system, if you must know). For example, I opted to study food and nutrition as one of my GCSEs and while I achieved a modest B grade I can, with hand on heart, say to you that the only thing I can effectively recall after two years and three ring binders' worth of nutritional study is that I don't want rickets. Why do I remember this above all else? Because I was privy to an extremely graphic picture of a man with a severe case of said ailment and I can clearly remember thinking, even back then, that it was not a good look.

So, we can see from the above that laughter brings with it a wealth of health benefits. But, in the words of Jimmy Cricket, there's more. Behold this list from 'Laughologist' Stephanie Davies detailing what is going on physically when we have a good old giggle (I have added the technical nitty-gritty in brackets).[1]

- A change in brain chemistry – happy chemicals as well as endorphins are released, including dopamine, which is a key learning chemical and improves our overall memory of what happened during and just before the event that made us laugh (handy).
- Scalp relaxes (reiki reiki, rise and shine!).
- Your head moves (lovely).
- Your eyebrows go up (unless you've had Botox).
- Your eyes widen (and sparkle).
- Your tears flow (I need tissues).

1 Davies, *Laughology*, pp. 42–43.

- Your nose crinkles and snorts (where are those tissues?).
- Snot runs down your nose (bugger).
- Your cheeks crease up and you smile (fifteen different muscles in the face alone are used when laughing).
- Ears go back (I can do this action at will – it's hereditary, though I like to think of it as a gift).
- Your face goes red (and in extreme cases purple!).
- Your mouth opens (and if you're my nan, no sound comes out, just silence and tears).
- Lips draw back into a smile (how many people do you know who swear that they are in a good mood but have somehow forgotten to tell their face!?).
- Tongue sticks out (how rude).
- Breath is expelled (minty fresh).
- You can cough (hand over your mouth, please).
- You can splutter (you should keep your spittle to yourself).
- You may make strange noises (snort, cackle, guffaw, bark, honk, screech, snigger, etc.).
- You may draw in deep breaths (breathe, dear, breathe).
- Your neck muscles relax (and, in some cases, a couple of chins).
- Your shoulders shake (feel the burn).
- Your chest swells (leave it).
- Your lungs expand (bloody hell).

- Your oxygen intake increases (hold on!).
- Your heart rate increases (don't panic!).
- Your heart muscles relax (aahh).
- Your blood vessels relax (that's better).
- Your belly wobbles (mine does this even when I'm not laughing).
- Your stomach muscles contract (yeah, whatever).
- You may break wind (and if you've had beans on toast for breakfast you may clear the room).
- Your hand grabs the belly (your own).
- You bend at the waist (yours, nobody else's).
- A bit of wee pops out (don't worry, I won't tell if you don't).
- Your knees bend.
- Your toes curl.
- Your whole body rocks.
- Ra ra ra!

Laughter is the best medicine, unless you've got syphilis, in which case penicillin is the best medicine.

ANONYMOUS

Maybe I was wrong about laughter making you more attractive, especially if all of this happens at once and you turn into a wheezing, snorting, shaky, snotty, incontinent lunatic. That's probably why they don't have singles nights at comedy clubs.

On top of this physiological impact, laughter and humour have a massive impact on how we receive and store information in that little grey noodle betwixt our ears. According to an article by Marshall Brain (I know!), founder of website HowStuffWorks, 'laughter seems to be produced via a circuit that runs through many regions of the brain'.[2]

Below is a quite literal 'brain' breakdown of which areas of our brain are utilised and engaged when we take a little trip to chuckledom:

- Left-side cortex (where the words and the structure of a joke are analysed).
- Frontal lobe (involved in our social and emotional responses).
- Right-side cortex (the intellectual analysis required to 'get' the joke occurs here. Occasionally non-responsive during my act).
- Sensory processing area of the occipital lobe (contains cells that process visual signals. Did I mention I was ginger?).
- Motor sections (evokes our physical responses to a joke – see the list on pages 35–37).

The frontal lobe helps to connect our thinking brain with our emotional brain. We know that the more personal the learning, the more it resonates with the learner, the more connections it makes within the brain and the more likely they are to remember it weeks, months, maybe years after it was first imparted and learned. There's nothing odd about that, just simple sticky learning doing what it does best, which is sticking.

---

2 M. Brain, How Laughter Works, HowStuffWorks.com (1 April 2000). Available at: http://science.howstuffworks.com/life/laughter.htm.

> *I used to think that the brain was the greatest organ in the human body, then I realised, 'Hey! Look what's telling me that!'*
>
> **EMO PHILIPS**

So humour, laughter and getting our brain firing in the best way for learning are all inextricably linked. Nowhere is this more so than in the case of the daddy of all learning-related neurochemicals: dopamine. This little beauty is a naturally occurring neurochemical which not only improves our memory for what was happening when the dopamine was released, it also, magically, improves our memory of what was happening in the 15 minutes or so prior to the release of the dopamine. The brain loves doing what it loves doing, so it makes sense to have some sort of mechanism that will help us remember what it was doing when it got to feel so good.

So, what is the mechanism for producing dopamine? It is quite simple really. Dopamine is produced through 'reward or the anticipation of reward'. That is to say, by doing something we like doing, or by simply knowing we are about to do something we like doing. And one of the things we really like doing is having a laugh. In other words, when we have fun or we know we are about to have fun, this wonder-drug goes to work helping to lay down learning pathways while also strengthening synaptic connections. This has made it an invaluable, almost magical, resource to anyone seeking to engage in the pursuit of playful learning. If standing up part way through the lesson and doing some sort of bizarre exercise makes you laugh, then that is going to have a positive effect on dopamine production, and thereby memory and learning.

This links back to Chapter 3. If we get someone emotionally involved in what we are doing, if we ensure they are happy and are enjoying the situation, and we are therefore enabling them to release the right chemicals, we get their attention. If we get their attention, then they will be able to learn and the behaviour will take care of itself. This is why we need to create an atmosphere of play, experimentation and fun so that the young minds in front of us can be relaxed, flexible and at their optimum plasticity.

> *I can't give you brains, but I can give you a diploma.*[3]
>
> ***THE WIZARD OF OZ***

There is a widely held belief that while laughter is an intensely pleasurable physical release, it is in fact a release of tension brought on by the discovery that a perceived threat is in fact not a threat at all. Let's face it, there can be all kinds of tension within a classroom situation – the biggest ones being that no one wants to be the first or get anything wrong. You know as well as I do that if you put your hand up and said something a bit blurrgh in a room full of your peers, you can almost guarantee that the very next day you'd find yourself at lunchtime, in a corner, on your own, eating your packed lunch and wondering where it all went wrong. Most people are so terrified of getting something wrong that they'd rather not risk it at all.

3 I have a diploma and it has no currency in the world whatsoever.

> *I quit school in the sixth grade because of pneumonia; not because I had it, but because I couldn't spell it.*
>
> ROCKY GRAZIANO

Fear is the biggest block to happiness and success, and this is why laughter is so important in learning; humour helps to convey a wide range of thoughts, feelings, opinions and subjects that we may find difficult to express in any other way. It has a mercurial way of getting straight to the heart of a subject or point, employing economy of language for maximum effect. How many times have you heard someone trying to express a point of view, only for someone else to interject with a perfectly observed one-liner that does all the work in half the time?

> *George Bernard Shaw: Have reserved two tickets for opening night. Come and bring a friend, if you have one.*
>
> *Winston Churchill: Impossible to come to first night. Will come to second night, if you have one.*

CHAPTER 5

YOUR FUNNY BONE IS CONNECTED TO YOUR, ER ...

> *A sense of humour is great – it goes a long, long way in a marriage.*
>
> CHRIS ROCK

So far we have looked at the huge impact that laughter and humour can play on the physiology, psychology and neurology of learners, so now would be a good opportunity to take a little breather and reflect upon the things in your own life that you find funny and that serve to elicit your own unexpected 'sudden glories' along the way.

As I have been up all night preparing the following comedy questionnaire, the least you can do is go through it and speculate, cogitate and ruminate on all things jesty and jokey.

DAVE'S COMEDY QUESTIONNAIRE[1]

1 What type of comedy actually makes you laugh? Sketch comedy, slapstick, wordplay, observational, surreal, one-liners, satire, sarcasm, toilet humour, innuendo?

1 That's me, not the TV channel where you can catch up with *Top Gear* from the 1980s.

2 When are *you* funny? At home, in the classroom, with friends, with other teachers, with your own kids, on your own (everyone's funnier on their own), with everyone, with strangers, whenever you have an audience, whenever you've had a drink (everyone's funnier after a drink)?

3 What was the last thing you laughed at and why?

4 What is the funniest thing that has ever happened to you in the classroom?

5 What is the funniest thing a pupil has said to you?

6 What is your funniest attribute? Your face, your voice, your clothing (if you don't find your clothing funny, just ask a teenager), your attitude, your language, your physicality, your catchphrases?

7 Who do you find funny? What is it they do that you find amusing?

8 How often do you think you are funny?

9 What do you think you do that is already funny?

10 How would being funnier affect you, the people around you and the place in which you work?

11 What three things could you do to bring more humour to your workplace?

12 If 'fun' were happening in your classroom, would you see it as a good thing or stamp it out like excitement when it starts to snow on a Tuesday afternoon in December?

13 When you are enjoying yourself how does it make you feel?

14 When others are enjoying themselves because of you (as opposed to 'at your expense') how do you feel?

15 When and where were you when you were having the most fun in your life?

16 Does enjoying yourself have an effect on the way you learn?

17 What lesson or subject do you remember most from when you were at school and why?

18 What three words would your students use to describe you?

19 If you could design the ultimate teacher, which six qualities would you deem the most important?

20 What advice would your 7-year-old self give you now about having fun?

21 Is there anything funny happening around you right now? If not, what could you do to create some mirth-making?

22 Do you know what kind of humour the students you work with enjoy? What makes them laugh? (Take my word for it: this is a conversation definitely worth having. The more you have in your 'comedy store', the better prepared you'll be.)

23 Are you in 'good humour' most of the time, some of the time, rarely, get out of my way you or I'll smack you?

24 When you wake up how do you feel about the day ahead?

25 When students enter your classroom what do you want them to think, feel and do?

26 When students leave your classroom what do you want them to think, feel and do?

27 What is the first thing you say to your learners when they enter your space?

28 What is the last thing you say to them when they leave your space?

29 What do your students do that makes you laugh? Do you encourage it?

And the final, million-dollar question:

30 If you were arrested for being funny, would there be enough evidence to convict you?

Comedians develop the skill of using humour as a lens through which they can examine all kinds of topics and observations about life, as well as subjects that may be otherwise unremarkable, unpleasant or just unfunny. Humour is the Philosopher's Stone that turns everyday lead into comedy gold. It makes the mundane, the awful, the sad or the embarrassing into something we can all laugh at and find funny. But using humour in this way is just a skill, something anyone can learn. Like emptying the dishwasher or changing your pants (not to be confused with changing the dishwasher and emptying your pants). We don't exit the womb as fully fledged comedians with the ability to spin amusing anecdotes and work rooms of people into convulsing, hysterical wrecks. Our sense of humour takes years to develop and mature, right from our earliest childhood experiences of being tickled and played with to our most recent experiences of paying money for the very same experience.

As we discovered earlier, our behaviour and the things we say, in turn, influence how others behave and respond to us. If we behave in a way others perceive as humorous, their response, which might be a smile or a laugh, will be understood as a positive reaction and will encourage us to repeat the behaviour. Like Pavlov's dog salivating at the ring of a bell. If something you say or do is met with a favourable reaction, in order to get that same response again you repeat the behaviour, and so on and so forth. This is how our sense of humour develops – our dopamine-soaked pathways are laid down and our appetite for dog biscuits increases.

We may not possess the ability to always see the humour in a situation as it occurs but, later on, we can distance ourselves and reflect on it, replaying the situation to see if we can find a humorous angle with which to view it. My favourite is playing my wedding video backwards and walking out of church a free man. Recognising what is funny and what will cause laughter in life takes an observant eye (the other eye is resting). Humour works best, then, when we can create a funny perspective on a familiar experience or around a common topic area.

> *So what if Jesus turned water into wine ... I turned a whole student loan into vodka once. Your move, Jesus ...*
>
> **SEAN LOCK**

As a teacher, making remarks about commonplace aspects of everyday life and learning can be a key skill to engage your audience. The premise of 'It's funny because it's true' applies because you are all singing from the same hysterical hymn sheet, and are running a funny situation up the comedy flagpole and saluting it together.

Peter Kay's depiction of parents of the future illustrates this beautifully.

> *You don't know you're born. All your mum and me used to have in the evenings was Sky Digital. PlayStation, yeah. We used to have to manage with a car each, a car each! Your*

> *mam, she used to have a dishwasher! You don't remember – look at her face, you don't remember them, do you? She used to have to take over all the plates, load them in, by hand, on her own! Turn it on!*[2]

This is your starting point then, that humour must be relevant to you all. To help and assist you to 'think funny' try using a 'comedy-gram'.[3] This is simply a tool to enable anyone to think about different topics and situations in a comedic light. Let me give you an example of how a comedy-gram might work – and let's use, I don't know, off the top of my head, choosing a topic at random, plucking an idea from the air, how about 'school' – and see what comedy observations we can make. (See figure on page 49.)

Now try adding your own observation in the empty box (I've provided some examples below but no peeking). What goes on at school that everyone will recognise, no matter what sort of school they went to, no matter how old they are, no matter where they're from? At this point don't try to be funny. Just remember the golden rule: sometimes things are funny just because they are true. Like Michael Gove, or any other politician come to think of it.

How did you get on? Here are some observations I prepared earlier. Don't worry if mine are better than yours – I am a professional.

- All the excuses you used for not having done your homework.
- Chewing gum under the desk.
- All the jiggery pokery that took place on school trips.
- The school disco with boys on one side and girls on the other, all waiting for Spandau Ballet's 'True' to come on.

---

2 P. Kay, *Live at the Top of the Tower* [DVD] (London: Universal Pictures UK, 2004).

3 Davies, *Laughology*, pp. 81–82.

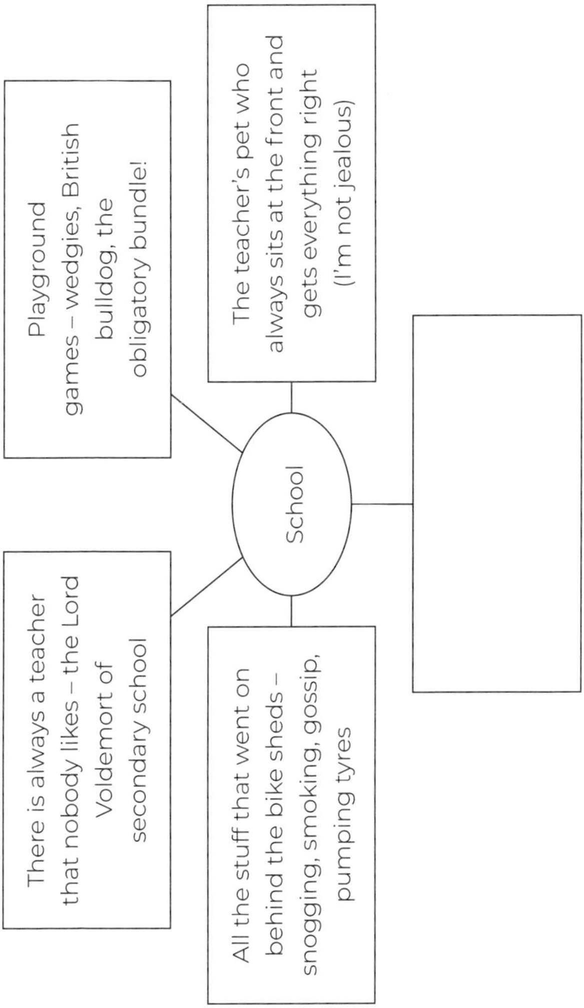
School
Playground games – wedgies, British bulldog, the obligatory bundle!
The teacher's pet who always sits at the front and gets everything right (I'm not jealous)
There is always a teacher that nobody likes – the Lord Voldemort of secondary school
All the stuff that went on behind the bike sheds – snogging, smoking, gossip, pumping tyres

- Dodgy haircuts.
- The smelly kid.
- School dinners.
- Nicknames.
- Changing the words to hymns.
- The many ways you discovered to make a supply teacher cry ...

> *The whole object of comedy is to be yourself, and the closer you get to that, the funnier you will be.*
>
> JERRY SEINFELD

Now you have the comedy-gram in your grab-bag of techniques, get your learners to do the graft. Next time you are starting a new topic, or itching to get a good debate going or would just like to know what is going on in the minds of young people, whack a theme in the middle and let the class riff away and see what they come up with. It will make the learning fun, create more laughs and will go a long way to aiding the recollection of content.

The comedy-gram is just one tool to help you put the 'agog' in pedagogy. Most comedians keep a notebook handy to jot down observations, ideas, comments, thoughts and words that have struck them as comical as they go about their daily lives. As an experiment over the next couple of weeks, make a list or keep a diary of the things that make you titter, snigger, guffaw and cackle. Record what it was and why you thought it was funny. Before you know it, you'll have a very handy reference-cum-source book of observations and ideas that will act as your guide on your journey towards the jocular.

CHAPTER 6

ONLY JOKING

> *My school days were the happiest days of my life, which should give you some indication of the misery I've endured over the past twenty-five years.*
>
> PAUL MERTON

Being humorous has a great deal to do with being open and spontaneous. It is about being alert to possibilities, to new combinations, to finding the unexpected in the commonplace as well as the unpredicted in the unexpected. That said, it is also imperative that we understand the setting in which we are using humour. The classroom isn't a late-night comedy club or an episode of *8 Out of 10 Cats*, so it is paramount when introducing humour into the classroom that a set of rules is established that everyone respects and adheres to. Be very clear: humour and laughter are not about saying what you want, when you want, to whom you want and then, when you upset someone, trying to get out of it by saying, 'I was only joking.' Never make it personal.

Below, for your delectation, is a shortlist of five key points that my mate and fellow comedian Stephanie Davies thinks you should consider when navigating the shark-infested custard of classroom humour, to which I've added some comic asides of my own.[1]

1 **Know your audience**

Aside: If you're going to engage in banter[2] with someone, be confident that you can gauge how they

1 Davies, *Laughology*, p. 48.

2 Or, as I like to call it, verbal tickling.

will take it. Like personal space, French kissing on a first date or car keys in the middle after dessert, everyone's boundaries are different, so please bear this in mind before you mentally scar someone for life.

2 **Leave serious topics alone**

Aside: If Bernard Manning is your comedy idol you probably shouldn't be let loose in a school environment, so may I suggest that you don't joke about contentious topics that may cause pain, embarrassment or upset to others. I, like Stephanie, would recommend you avoid joking about death, sexual harassment, physical disability, mental disability or race. Even the Germans. Save all of these for your family after the Queen's Speech at Christmas. And while we're on this subject, I would steer well clear of using other teachers or students for the purposes of your comic radar too.

3 **Be careful of politics and religion**

Aside: Talking of subjects to avoid, humour should never be used as a divisive tool and so I recommend that you should give a very wide berth to any topic that could potentially single out an individual or group or undermine someone's beliefs or value system. This is really hard to do when a student starts quoting the *Daily Mail* at you but, come on son, leave it, it's not worth it ...

4 **If in doubt, leave it out**

Aside: If you think for a moment that your idea may have a good chance of dying on its backside, or indeed upsetting half your school-based congregation, then I suggest you put it to one side and leave it there. Remember, humour is very much like toothpaste or a comment on Twitter – once it's out there, it's out there. You can't take it back.

5 **Smile and enjoy yourself**

Aside: You'd be surprised how many people forget to do this. Unless you're going for the Jack Dee approach, make sure everyone knows you're having a laugh and that it's good for you and quite safe.

You may wish to enlist the creative input of your class in the production of a 'Humour Rules' board. If you create a set of guidelines together and decide on the repercussions should any of the rules be broken, it is more likely that the students will stick to them and they will utilise humour in the learning environment with the respect and positivity that it deserves.

> *Well, I was bullied at school, called all kinds of different names. But one day I turned to my bullies and said, 'Sticks and stones may break my bones but names will never hurt me' – and it worked! From there on it was sticks and stones all the way.*
>
> HARRY HILL

COMIC ASIDE: FIVE GREAT HUMOUR TRICKS

While I'm all for spontaneity when it comes to humour, there are certain tricks and techniques that are great fall-backs and that will never cease to come up trumps in getting people curious, giggling and learning. Here are five easy wins for the comedy classroom.

1. SURPRISE

Introduce an element of surprise into the classroom (or indeed the bedroom), as it does four things:

i It wakes up all parties as it changes the direction of where everyone thought they were going, even if in just a small way.

ii It helps to keep everyone alert.

iii It injects a sense of fun and humour into proceedings. Indeed, surprise is an important ingredient for laughter and humour. It is often the shock, the unexpected moment within a situation, that makes us laugh – the bisociation that we met earlier.

iv It can be a way of checking if everyone is paying attention. By adding in something completely unexpected, the students should pick up on it – if they're listening! If not, you need to add in more and bigger surprises.

I'll never forget the day that my history teacher, Mr Matthews, turned up to a lesson wearing a Ronald Reagan mask. Not particularly groundbreaking now, perhaps, but at the time (1988 – a year when *Red Dwarf* and *Cannon and Ball* vied for our comedy attention on the telly) this was seen as a miracle of comedic invention. The funniest thing about the whole experience was that he never did 'the reveal'. You would think that at some point during the session he would have peeled back the mask to reassure the class that it was in fact Mr Matthews and not some deranged passer-by with a penchant for rubber masks and Notts schoolchildren. For all we knew it could have been the real Ronald Reagan under the mask. No one would have expected that! But we all thought he was completely mental and would queue for his lessons just to see what he would do next. Mr Matthews didn't do bizarre things every lesson, but he would throw in a curveball every now and again, just to keep us on our toes. More than 30 years later, I am telling you about it as one of my abiding memories of school. Now that's what I call high-impact learning.

Pupil: I don't think I deserved zero on this test.

Teacher: I agree, but that's the lowest mark I could give you.

2. EXAGGERATION

This is a brilliant strategy for improving memory. We don't think only in words, but most of us will revise a topic in that way. If I asked you to visualise a cow, you wouldn't picture a piece of paper in your head with the word 'cow' written on it – you would see a picture of a cow. You've probably gone for a traditional black-and-white cow but if I said make it blue, give it a curly wig and have it tap dance while belting out a jazz hands version of 'Don't Rain on My Parade', that would be a cow to remember. We need to really help our students to magnify their learning in this way, especially for the bits that aren't as 'sticky' as others. The more they get used to playing with the information, and the more magnified and exaggerated the work is, the better chance that piece of knowledge has of standing out and being recollected at a later date. What elements of your lessons can be exaggerated to great educational effect?

Good teaching is one fourth preparation and three fourths theatre.

GAIL GODWIN

3. SILLINESS

Knowing yourself and being confident enough in your own skin to send yourself up and to say and do things out of the ordinary or that may be seen as ridiculous, shows a strong sense of character and good self-esteem. Silliness can immediately take away the seriousness of a situation, highlight other situations/key points and can help navigate moments that may otherwise cause anxiety. Remember that 'anxiety is simply excitement without breath' and having a laugh means we're going to have to breathe sooner or later. Of course, through all of this it is vital to remember that the secret of good comed ... timing!

There are three kinds of people: those who can count and those who can't.

GEORGE CARLIN

4. STORY

For centuries, storytelling – and the tricks used therein such as metaphor and simile – has been a vital tool in the passing on of ideas, knowledge and wisdom. In the classroom, apart from the open fire and someone with a guitar singing 'Kumbaya, my lord', it's no different. Stories, be they your own or from elsewhere, should be used as often as possible to bring the learning alive and make it real and relevant. The funnier the story, the better.

We've been sitting here since Christmas 1914, during which time millions of men have died, and we've advanced no further than an asthmatic ant with some heavy shopping.

BLACKADDER, *BLACKADDER GOES FORTH*

5. IMAGINATION

The great thing about imagination is you can't get it wrong; it's simply what you think and no one can take that away from you. Try not to let your inner editor stop you from being free in your thinking. Do you ever feel like your first thought isn't good enough and you should think of something better? Remember, anything goes. Sometimes the most bizarre situations and the strangest and darkest parts of your imagination can conjure up the funniest things. Don't get trapped by your day-to-day reality. Be open and let your imagination run amok, before your students do.

Three blind mice walk into a pub. But they are all unaware of their surroundings, so to derive humour from it would be exploitative.

BILL BAILEY

CHAPTER 7

PLEASE BE SEATED FOR THE SECRETS OF STAND-UP

When people are laughing they're generally not killing each other.

ALAN ALDA

Standing up in a roomful of complete strangers and attempting to make them laugh is most people's second worst nightmare, only beaten by doing it naked. But if that's the only way you can get a quick laugh (and at some events I still do), then so be it.

As a stand-up comedian, I have spent many a glorious evening in a decaying pub beneath an underpowered, flickering spotlight on a blood-soaked stage gazing out on an audience of eight knuckle-scraping inbreds and wondering whether I should have joined my dad and gone into insurance. But then, despite all the odds, people laugh – and when you can keep a roomful of strangers in fits of laughter for 20 minutes, there is nothing quite like it in the world.

In all my years in education, and especially during the times I have been faced with 400 Year 11 boys for two hours straight on a Friday afternoon, boys who have just been told they can't do PE,[1] I have drawn on every stand-up trick in the book to question, engage, probe, push, prod, meddle, cajole and banter in order to pull it off/get out alive.

1 True story!

While I could just show you a photo album of my scars, a far better use of your time will be for me to share with you the 20 best stand-up tips that I feel could be beneficial in a classroom context and could lead to many moments of learning-centred mirth. Brace yourself ...

1. THE RULE OF THREE

This is a comedy stalwart and is as old as time itself. Whenever you are thinking of deploying the rule of three, the best advice to remember is this:

Establish – reinforce – twist

So, an example of this could be:

> *My wife is the light of my life, the apple of my eye, the pain in my arse.*

What is happening here, apart from the early tell-tale signs of divorce, is that the first two statements establish a pattern that the last one then breaks. It is that break, again that bisociation, which produces the humour and gets the giggles going. Once you are familiar with the pattern you can use lots of different ones, such as these categories suggested by humour specialist John Kindes on his website www.humorpower.com, which could be used like this:

Ordinary – ordinary – ridiculous:

> *On our last holiday we got sand, sea and septicaemia.*
>
> *When you've done the work you can either pack your stuff away quietly, leave two minutes early or be tickled till you're sick.*

Expected trait – expected trait – unexpected trait:

> *He had the patience of a saint, the voice of an angel, and the body of a truck driver.*

She was loud, lascivious, and a librarian.

Same category – same category – different category:

For Valentine's Day I got flowers, chocolates and a restraining order.

He could sell a burger to a vegetarian, holy water to an atheist and a pound of crystal meth to his gran. (I've been watching too much Breaking Bad*).*

Something everyone loves – something everyone loves – something everyone hates:

Hands up if you want to be successful? Hands up if you want to be happy? Hands up if you want to be a maths teacher?

I love hard-hitting TV. Panorama. Newsnight. Hollyoaks.

Extreme – extreme – ordinary:

As I gazed into his eyes I could see evil, hatred and the reflection from Specsavers' window.

The alien had three heads, huge claws and a lovely smile.

It is the rhythm that makes this work so well and it is a very useful technique to keep in your educator's funny-bag. The next time you're asking the class a question, make the third part to it something unexpected. Or when you do a quiz, you could have multiple-choice answers with the third choice being the twist. A friend of mine used to give the following question to his French students:

If the French for 'babysitting' is 'le babysitting' and the French for 'weekend' is 'le weekend', what's the French for 'combine harvester'?[2]

Once you look you'll start to see that there are many applications for this technique – and the more you do it, the

2 It's *moissonneuse-batteuse* in case you were wondering. They never got it right!

more quickly you will see opportunities to drop them in without having to think too much about it in advance.

2. GIVE IT BACK/HECKLE

Be careful here not to confuse heckling with a put-down. Let's try to keep away from offensive and hurtful put-downs, at least in the classroom anyway. Usually we don't respond to a heckle straight away as we are worried about not appearing funny. But here's the secret – you don't have to be funny! Yes, all this time you thought handling a heckler was a brilliantly clever thing to do, but no, it's just responding quickly and generally with anything that is appropriate at the time. In everyday life we respond to conversations in an off-the-cuff way without being highly prepared, so do this with heckles or shout-outs. It will get you thinking quicker and show you are confident in handling what people throw at you.

Here are four classic heckle responses for your delectation:

> *Heckler: I met you at medical school.*
>
> *Frank Skinner: Ah, yes. You were the one in the jar.*
>
> *John Cooper Clarke: Your bus leaves in ten minutes ... Be under it.*
>
> *Richard Herring: If you're going to heckle, try and wait for there to be a gap when I'm not speaking, so people can hear what you're saying ... So if you're going to come and heckle, at least come prepared. Don't get so drunk you can't think, that's the first rule of heckling. The second rule: maybe your own amplification system of some kind.*
>
> *Harry Hill: You might heckle me now – but when I get home I've got a chicken in the oven.*

To a roomful of independent school sixth-formers:

Me: Anyone here take food technology at GCSE?

The room replies in a mocking snort, 'no'.

Me: No, well you've probably got staff for that.

But what about those situations where you've just been heckled and you find yourself standing there with your mind as empty as a parents' evening on a Champions League night? The best advice I can give you is actually quite straightforward – simply repeat what you have just heard. Not only does this ensure those who weren't listening know what was said, it also, more importantly, gives you a brief but critical moment to think. During this time you can come up with something witty or create a way to bring the comment and/or person delivering it into the lesson. A lot of people will look upon an interruption as a disturbance – and while some are, and should be dealt with swiftly, others can be very useful and revealing in terms of the thought processes of your students with regards to the content or delivery of a lesson.

Let me illuminate my point with a very recent experience I had while delivering a secondary school INSET day somewhere off the M4. I had just asked the room to come up with three things they felt would make the day enjoyable.

Me: Who would like to share one thing that will make the day enjoyable? How about you, sir? (Seeking to engage the audience from the off)

Man in second row: I want you to tell me something I don't know! (Seeking to annoy the presenter from the off)

Me: Tell you something you don't know, eh? (Repeating back to provide a moment's thought) OK, you tell me everything you know and then I'll tell you something you don't know!

At this point, the room erupts in laughter as the man in the second row realises that his suggestion was ill thought out, a waste of everyone's time and that the guy at the front is a seasoned professional used to dealing with awkward buggers of all shapes and sizes.

3. KNOW YOUR AUDIENCE

> *I've created an atmosphere where I'm a friend first, boss second. Probably entertainer third.*
>
> **DAVID BRENT, *THE OFFICE***

Getting to know people in your class/audience is incredibly important if you want to form positive relationships. But it's not just their names, which in most cases you've got a year to remember. It could be nicknames, whether they are in a band, if they play football, what TV they watch or whether they are in a relationship. It's what good MCs do in comedy clubs every night of the week. It's what the 'Anyone here from Wales?' routine or 'Any teachers in the audience? Don't shout out!' line is all about. All of this is a great advantage to you as a teacher when looking for ways to link the learning in the lesson to them as individuals, to make it real and to connect with the young minds in front of you. The secret is to look at everything that is said or occurs in your lesson as useful. Nothing should ever be wasted. To help with this, you could suggest that the students all make a badge with their chosen nickname on it or emblazoned with a favourite pastime, band, film or food. Anything and everything that you could find useful in getting to know them, so that you can deftly link the learning to them as people.

4. AUDIENCE PARTICIPATION

I won't say ours was a tough school, but we had our own coroner. We used to write essays like: What I'm going to be if I grow up.

LENNY BRUCE

Wherever and whenever it is possible, audience participation is vital in bringing the lesson to life and hardwiring the learning into the students' heads. We now know that we all have access to what is called 'muscle memory', the ability to remember something by doing it, as opposed to only hearing or seeing it. I also now know, due to years of travelling up and down the country working with all kinds of learners, that drawing on an audience in this way can create some of the most funny and memorable experiences you will ever have in a learning context.

A good teacher, like a good comic, should always be aware of what their audience is doing at all times. Are they engaged and, if not, can I be flexible enough in the moment to tailor my lesson to fit the needs of all those gathered before me? Can I get them back on track with a question they weren't expecting? Can I bring them in with a well-crafted change in direction, tone, thought or activity? Your audience is the sole reason you are there so, whether they are captive or not, they need to feel wanted, valued and a necessary part of the ongoing action of a lesson.

Humour generates social bonding and as long as that grows, so will your relationships with the people in front of you. Which bits of your lesson could the students lead or at least take part in? Could one of them introduce the key theme of the lesson or come prepared with a list of five things they've researched about the topic? Could they mark each other's work? Could they act out or debate any relevant questions, themes or events? The less you do, the more they can do.[3] The students you work with are clever enough to educate each other, honest!

> *But with comedy it's a simple premise. If it's funny, people laugh. If it's not, they don't.*
>
> STEVE COOGAN

5. ATTITUDE

> *I kept on getting into trouble at school for handing my homework in late, so I bought a book of excuses. Unfortunately, the dog ate it.*
>
> ANONYMOUS

Comedian Logan Murray, who has imparted much about the philosophy of comedy through his stand-up comedy courses for Amused Moose, is quoted in Steve Jacobi's book *Laughing Matters* as saying: 'Let your mind go. Being funny is as much a state of mind as anything else. You should never be thinking, how can I please an audience? Instead, you should impose yourself and believe what you want to say is funny.'[4]

3 You really need to check out Jim Smith's *Lazy Teacher's Handbook – New Edition* (2017) for more of this sort of stuff – priceless.

4 S. Jacobi, *Laughing Matters* (London: Arrow Books/Random House, 2005), p. 93.

How do you wish to be viewed by your class? Somebody once said that teaching is a form of interruption, so if you are going to interrupt the lives of your students, it had better be for a good reason. If you impose yourself, how do you want that imposition to be remembered? I was recently asked to observe a lesson (or watch a teacher cope for 50 minutes, depending on your point of view). At the end of the session, I was then asked by a friend to jot down a sentence that summed up what I had just witnessed so he was able to feed back to the teacher in question. My sentence simply read: 'The children did not care enough about the person in front of them to do as they asked.'

If you feel the need to boil down teaching to something, then boil it down to that. It is imperative that, as a leader in the classroom, you remain relaxed, confident and approachable at all times. Students love a teacher who is self-deprecating in a humorous (as opposed to suicidal) manner. It shows a different and more human side to a person who some students believe actually lives at school and has no friends. Teachers who use humour can come across to young people as more enthusiastic and therefore engaging. It's all about attitude. So, if attitude is infectious, make sure yours is worth catching.

6. PHYSICALITY

While I am not advocating a quick course in the art of slapstick (although never underestimate how funny falling over can be) it is worth mentioning that what you do physically in a classroom, and how that makes others feel, can massively reinforce everything you are saying. If only a portion of what we take away from engaging with someone is the actual words (we don't remember every word that was ever said to us but we do remember or have a sense of how someone made us feel), then what we do with our voice, the emotion we invest in that communication and the way we deliver it physically can all play an important role in how it is received and, crucially, remembered. Where you stand, what you stand on (what you stand in – that's slapstick for you!), where and how you direct the students' attention and how you use the space around you – all of these factors can and should form part of your everyday comedic kitbag. How can you best utilise the space in which you work? Is there somewhere you can stand specifically when delivering a key piece of information? The 'Crucial Corner'? Can you play with levels, standing somewhere higher for maximum effect or crouching lower to draw everyone in so that the students know they must remember it and give it the attention it deserves?

> *Comedy comes from inside. It comes from your face. It comes from your body.*
>
> **HAROLD LLOYD**

7. BEING OPEN

> *What's another word for thesaurus?*
>
> **STEVEN WRIGHT**

Openness is the key to creativity and so much of what this book is aiming to do is to get you, dear reader, to welcome in the joy of laughter, humour and creativity through the revolving door of openness. Leave all your adult fears, anxieties, prejudices, hang-ups and supposed shortage of confidence behind you when you leave the house each day, and embrace your new-found freedom as you wander the realms of possibility, opportunity and fun. Humour has a way of disarming us. It seems to prevent people from attacking ideas. It encourages and supports a more receptive frame of mind and, in doing so, inspires a willingness to contribute.

8. MAKE IT A GAME

> *As you get older you're told to be sensible, but it's important for writing if you're a comic that you're able to still access that childlike thing.*
>
> TIM VINE

Work less, play more. There, I've said it. It's not a throwaway comment or an airy-fairy notion but quite simply an order. Stop working so hard and give yourself permission to have a ball. Remember our friend neoteny from Chapter 3? Playing promotes curiosity, open-mindedness, imagination and improved thinking. Einstein used his playful thoughts – his thought experiments – to think about how the universe really works. So, go on, tune in and drop out into the world of play. You deserve it. How can you play with the learning – mess about with it so it doesn't feel like work – yet the outcome takes care of itself? Ask the students how they would approach a piece of work if they were allowed to muck about with it as much as they liked but without losing sight of the learning goal.

9. DON'T TRY TOO HARD

You know how to tell if the teacher is hungover? Movie Day.

JAY MOHR

As anyone knows who has ever watched the 'auditions' episodes of *Britain's Got Talent*, there is nothing worse than the whiff of desperation. Individuals who are trying so hard that they've forgotten not only who they are but also that they need to engage with the people directly in front of them are an ordeal to watch. This is not about throwing everything you've ever known out of the window and starting from scratch. This is about refining the skills you already have within you and your working practice. All good stand-ups are constantly honing and reworking their sets until they have what we call a 'bulletproof act'. Comedian Frank Skinner once said that if you have a strong opening and a strong finish, the middle will take care of itself (if you don't believe me, ask my wife!). What this means is that you can try out new material in the middle because you already know you've got them eating out of the palm of your hand, and even if this new bit of the routine doesn't work too well, at least you know you've got that big finish that'll knock 'em off their feet and leave 'em wanting more.[5]

5 And leaving 'em wanting more is another golden rule when it comes to keeping people engaged, as P. T. Barnum knew so well. Remember that as you plan the end of your lessons.

10. DON'T BE AFRAID TO FAIL

I took a physics course that was so hard I couldn't find the classroom.

STEVE CONNELLY

Every comic who has ever stood up has fallen flat on their arse at least once, if not multiple times, during their career. The first quality you learn as a stand-up is to develop a very thick skin. And a bouncy arse. But it is also very much about looking at each gig (or lesson) as an opportunity to learn, develop and improve. You are, as they say, only as good as your last job. It doesn't matter how funny you were last week in Swindon, it's how funny you're going to be tonight in Lichfield (I get to go to all the best places). It's the same with a class. It doesn't matter how good the lesson was last week when you had them hanging on your every word with your incredible introspective on the life-cycle of a frog; it's your performance when you deliver the next lesson that counts. So, knowing that you will fail at least some of the time, don't sweat it. Just keep trying new stuff out. Nobody dies. You'll never know whether it works or not if you don't give it a whirl. Try it out, cock it up, then try it differently. If it doesn't work a third time, let it go and move on. Life's too short. Life and learning is an ongoing, evolutionary developmental process: a constant, iterative chipping away to reveal new things about ourselves, the people around us and the places we find ourselves in. Don't waste that gift trying to be perfect all the time.

11. SELL IT AND SELL IT HARD

There are times when you have to fall back on one special rule – use everything you've ever known and use it now. In his book *Born Standing Up: A Comic's Life*, Steve Martin talks about having to use everything he'd got in his locker at some point in front of an audience.[6] I know for a fact that I've had to call upon all kinds of gifts, quirks, skills, talents and foibles during my educational and artistic careers. Everything from juggling, beatboxing, pulling funny faces, falling over, drumming, dancing, falling over again, magic, card tricks, pulling funny faces while drumming, dancing and falling over – absolutely anything and everything that I felt might help inspire, amuse, befuddle, shock, enthral, enthuse or entertain while I sought to educate. No amount of positive effort is ever wasted, no matter how small or insignificant it appears at the time. What have *you* got up your sleeve when the time comes?

12. TIMING

My father wanted me to have all the opportunities he never had, so he sent me to a girls' school.

JACK HERBERT

In the classroom, you choose how the time is spent – and these choices can make or break a session. It has been reported that when students first enter a lesson, their ability to receive and store information is as high as 98%. This is most probably due to the fact that they've just been outside for some fresh air, ingested a week's supply of

6 S. Martin, *Born Standing Up: A Comic's Life* (New York: Pocket Books, 2008).

sugary snacks and are now waiting with anticipation for some golden nuggets of knowledge from you. But it doesn't take too long before their ability to receive and store information quickly plummets, their focus begins to wander and their concentration wanes.

Have you ever been in a lesson when someone walks past the window and this moment is met with the same interest and excitement as if dinosaurs once again stalked the earth? But the opposite happens towards the end of the lesson. Now, concentration and focus levels rise rapidly, even if it is only that the students are beginning to imagine what gastronomic delights or gossip awaits them in the canteen at lunchtime. What will help therefore are more beginnings and ends in each lesson and a much less boring middle. (*James Bond* directors are you listening?) So, hit the stop/start button more often. Every time you change direction in a lesson, you are re-firing the brains of the students in front of you, be it with an activity, discussion, plenary or technical intervention. The way you run your session is as important as the content. Keep on your toes to keep them on theirs.

13. RIFFING

This is the ability to explore an idea, go where it goes, build off other people's input and see where that takes you. It's like a mental version of the comedy-gram. It's a way of working that gets all kinds of neurological connections firing and promotes the art of 'first thoughts'. Yep, you heard me. Saying the first thing that comes into your head and going with it is an art. Trust me! (More on this in Chapter 8.) The great thing about riffing is this: if it works, make a note and keep it in for next time, and if it doesn't work, get rid and pretend it never happened. Riffing helps to build up content, ideas and thoughts and helps to develop great working relationships.

I am so clever that sometimes I don't understand a single word of what I am saying.

OSCAR WILDE

14. CONFIDENCE

Smartness runs in my family. When I went to school I was so smart my teacher was in my class for five years.

GRACIE ALLEN

Confidence is key. The word 'confidence' comes from the Latin meaning to 'have full trust'. Unfortunately, we've got confidence wrong. Most people think you get confident first and that then you go and do something. But that, like the Star Wars movie *The Phantom Menace*, which is the fourth film in the series but is actually Episode 1, is arse about face. You don't get confident and do it; you do it and then you get confident. Confidence comes after the experience, not before it – as a result of that experience. That's why everything in this book, indeed in my life, is about having a go. Do it, gain the experience, feel the burn, get the confidence.

Am I jumping the gun, Baldrick, or are the words 'I have a cunning plan' marching with ill-deserved confidence in the direction of this conversation?

EDMUND, *BLACKADDER THE THIRD*

15. FEEDBACK

In school I wanted to join the debating team ... but someone talked me out of it.

STEWART FRANCIS

Many comics will record their sets so that when they get home they can replay it and see what worked, what needs reworking and what needs dumping. The good news is that you don't need to do this as you have a ready-made feedback system called 'students'. Students are often an incredibly undervalued resource when it comes to exploring what works and what doesn't. Never forget that they've had the pleasure/misfortune of sitting through hundreds of lessons and are adept at knowing what worked, what didn't and, crucially, why. If you don't feel brave enough to engage the whole group in feedback, then maybe address a select few at the end of the lesson or do what I do and ask them halfway through to make sure that everyone is on board and happy to carry on. 'Is this working for you?' is a much underused question in so many areas of life (although it can spoil the mood at times). While some of the feedback we receive may be hard to take, it is imperative for our own personal growth that we learn to use it as a way of moving forward and not as a big stick with which to beat ourselves around the proverbial head.

16. DARE TO BE DIFFERENT

I speak 12 languages. English is the bestest.

STEFAN BERGMAN

This isn't a cliché. Well, OK, it is. But that doesn't make it any less true when it comes to mining for comedy gold. Different is good. If we didn't do anything different, nothing would change. Nothing would develop or evolve. Nothing would happen. We all need to be daring, and your students will get the green light for this to take place from you. There is a lovely saying which goes like this: 'Find out what's unique about you and sell it back to the world.' Everyone has a unique trait, skill, attribute or quality that makes them great. What's yours? And if you don't know, ask around and find out. Be faithful to yourself.

The richest kind of laughter is the laughter in response to things people would ordinarily never laugh at.

BILL HICKS

17. FLIP PERSPECTIVES

Of course I knew that knickers began with a K. I've been to Oxford – it's one of the first things they teach you.

ALAN BENNETT

This is simply to get used to looking at things from a different angle. It's what good stand-ups are great at and it's this 'flip' on reality that creates the laughter. Below is an exercise I use a lot with staff to help illustrate my flipping point.

Get a group to pick three people who are currently in the public eye and then ask how things would change if they were in charge of education or a particular lesson. For instance, recent popular choices have included Boris Johnson, Jessica Ennis-Hill and Hugh Jackman (my wife made me put him in). What skills, attributes and qualities have these three got that they could bring to the table and apply in order to change education?

Looking at things from a different vantage point allows us to refresh our own point of view, as well as give us a method for generating new thoughts, feelings and ideas.

18. CALLBACK

In comedy, a 'callback' is a joke or comment that refers back to a previous joke or comment in the set that worked. For instance, when I'm performing/working I may ascertain early on who the naughtiest person in the room is. This means that whenever something vaguely naughty occurs or is said or hinted at, I can comment, look at, refer to or give a nod towards that person – something that will almost certainly get a laugh of recognition. The skill is to set up something in advance, such as a word/phrase, activity or relationship within the lesson that you can keep coming back to or refer to throughout the session. This will not only elicit a laugh but will also ensure the students remember it. It might even become a catchphrase, so just say what you see ...

19. GET YOURSELF A GIG

There will always be open-mic nights going on at a pub or club in your area. Ring up and book yourself in for a five-minute slot. The worst-case scenario is that, as at an after-dinner speech I once did in a revolving restaurant in Center Parcs for a group of drunk and moody head teachers, no one laughs. But hey, no one dies either. Including you. What's more, once you've faced an open-mic audience you realise how lovely that bottom set, Year 9 group really is. The best-case scenario is that you say something you have thought up all by yourself and a real bona-fide paying audience laughs at it and, for a moment, the world stops spinning and you realise there's a place in it just for you. And, you know what, joking aside, it feels fricking fantastic!

20. AFTERTHOUGHT

It is also worth mentioning the term 'afterthought', which is the name given to funny comments or quips which are made immediately after something has been said. For a better idea of what an afterthought is, or how to make one, please refer to anything in this book which appears in (brackets)! See what I did there? I put the word (brackets) in (brackets).

CHAPTER 8

MAKING IT UP AS YOU GO - IMPROVISATION AND TEACHING

Comedy is simply a funny way of being serious.

PETER USTINOV

It has been said that, when it comes to teaching, the secret is to appear to have known all your life what you have just learned this morning. There are many times during a school day when it feels exactly like this is what you're doing, despite the efforts you may have put into planning your lesson.

Improvisation – responding to what is going on in the moment and using it to make things better – has to be one of the most important skills a teacher has in their repertoire. That wonderful ability to think on your feet and to respond without the benefit of planning – or maybe despite the benefit of planning – because you never quite know how your audience will react or even what mood they will turn up in.

Spontaneity in our approach is crucial if we are to tap into our learners' love of play and excitement for the unknown. Keith Johnstone suggests in his seminal book *Impro: Improvisation and the Theatre*: 'Most children can operate in a creative way until they're eleven or twelve, when suddenly they lose their spontaneity and produce imitations of "adult art"'.[1]

Nurturing students' ability to improvise through our own ability to be spontaneous is not only good in the classroom but also helps them to develop soft skills for life, such as bravery, openness, communication, listening, decision making, creativity, energy, humour, whole-brain thinking, wit, laughter and self-expression. Where does that list show up on your exam certificate? The thing is, not many educational establishments are set up to promote this way of thinking and being. In fact, it could be argued that they are actually set up to stifle many of them.

Keith Johnstone backs up this point rather emphatically when he writes:

> *Many teachers think of children as immature adults. It might lead to better and more 'respectful' teaching, if we thought of adults as atrophied children. Many 'well adjusted' adults are bitter, uncreative, frightened, unimaginative and rather hostile people. Instead of assuming that we were born that way, or that that's what being an adult entails, we might consider them as people damaged by their education and upbringing.*[2]

We don't want generations of young people leaving education constrained by the experience and unable to access their inner creator. It's not fearful young people we need but fearless ones.

By its very definition, improvisation requires a fearlessness to constantly enter unfamiliar situations and scenarios where we don't know what the outcome will be; to frequently experience the feeling of going from conscious

1 K. Johnstone, *Impro: Improvisation and the Theatre* (London: Methuen Drama, 1989), p. 77.

2 Johnstone, *Impro*, p. 78.

incompetence to conscious competence; from not-knowing to knowing. This is similar to the feeling most students experience every time they enter a lesson.

The world of the 21st century is uncertain and full to the brim with constant change. If we want our young people to enjoy it rather than merely cope with it – or worse, not cope – then we must lead them in the development of bravery, self-expression, spontaneity and quick thinking. Below is a list of the top six things I believe are required to be a great improviser.

1. YES AND ...

Responding to every suggestion put to you with these two words can be very powerful. No matter what comes your way you are not only accepting it – 'Yes', you are adding to it – 'And'. For example, I say to you, 'Would you like to go to the pub?' and you say, quick as a flash, 'Yes, and I'll get the first round in.' This example works better in my dreams than it does in reality because you could equally well reply, 'Yes, and remember to bring your disguise so they'll let you back in.' (This idea links to the art of riffing as mentioned in Chapter 7.) As improv guru Keith Johnstone points out: 'There are people who prefer to say "Yes" and there are people who prefer to say "No". Those who say "Yes" are rewarded by the adventures they have and those who say "No" are rewarded by the safety they attain'.[3]

3 Johnstone, *Impro*, p. 92.

2. ADD NEW INFORMATION/ PROVIDE DETAILS/BRING SOMETHING TO THE TABLE

As in the previous example, improv only works if you're looking to keep it going and move it forward. When you receive new information, always seek to build on it, never destroy it. For instance, an exchange could be built like this:

> *Person 1: I have a bike.*
>
> *Person 2: Yes and it's big, black and only has one wheel, which is flat.*
>
> *Person 1: Yes and I would like you to help me pump it up using this new and improved industrial wonder pump.*
>
> *Person 2: Yes and I could grab you from behind to help with the pumping.*
>
> *Person 1: Yes and if that goes well we can get married.*
>
> *Person 2: Yes and then we can do all the things that people do when they get old and infirm.*
>
> *Person 1: Yes and we shall live happily ever after in a bungalow with our own teeth, an electric blanket and a cockapoo [that's a dog not a scatological parrot].*

You get the idea. The extra information and detail helps to build a bigger, better and more imaginative landscape in which the improvisers can work and explore.

Being able to constantly take on board information – to use it, build on it and send it back out better than before – is a very life-affirming skill to develop and has numerous benefits beyond the classroom. So many students develop what is called 'learned helplessness', where they will happily stick their hands in the air, sit back and wait for the adult in the room to give them the answer. In fact, I know a lot of grown-ups who are still waiting for the adult in the room to give them the answer. Life doesn't really work like that, which is why improv is so great for developing personal and group responsibility and turning every interaction into a positive one.

3. DON'T BLOCK!

Negativity will always get in the way of a good time and should not be tolerated! Blocking comes in many forms in improvisation, so the best rule to remember is to always 'go' with what someone has offered you. For example, if someone is improvising a scene where they come into your shop to buy a bike and you say, 'Excuse me, but this isn't a bike shop,' then that is blocking and you will be immediately sent to comedy hell. As will your audience. A better response would be: 'Yes, this is a bike shop, despite the absence of bikes, and, in actual fact, I have a special offer on today – if you buy a bike with one wheel then you get the other wheel free.' The way the likes of Paul Merton and other professional improvisers make it look so easy and slick is because they accept what is given to them and build on it. You can, of course, change the direction of the conversation, but the key here is that it is never at the expense of your fellow improviser. I would go as far as to say that this is a great rule for life in general – build on what people offer you and keep your contributions positive.

4. GO TO THE NTH DEGREE

In order to become independent learners who are never scared to express themselves, our students need to have the opportunity to push their boundaries, take risks and be courageous. Which means so do we. Be bold in your thinking and aim to get a strong reaction from your class to the learning taking place. The stronger the reaction, the better the recall and behaviour. If we go too far, at least we can reel it back in. Remember, if your reaction to learning involves any of the following – ooooooh, aaaaaaah, uuuuuuuurgh or phwoar – you are much more likely to recall it.

5. ENERGY

Good improvisers attack every thought, idea or action with 100% conviction that it will work. Sometimes the sheer force of that energy can turn something seemingly ordinary into something extraordinary. That's how diamonds are formed after all.

6. IT JUST POPPED RIGHT OUT

OK, so here's the biggest secret to being a good improviser. Are you ready for this? Here it comes ... just say anything! Yes, it's that simple. Saying the first thing that comes into your head is usually the right thing to say. It's just having the confidence to say it. What happens instead most of the time is that we go through life being taught to edit ourselves – look before you leap, think before you open your mouth, don't do that to your nan. Of course, we need to have self-awareness for social situations and an understanding of etiquette. But in improvisation different rules apply and you can and should turn off your edit button. As long as you are using good humour and playing within the improv rules, then the funny comes from the first thought that pops into your head. The more absurd the better! Try it now. Just say the first thing in your head (you may wish to make sure you're on your own if this is your first time). It may reveal more about you and your thoughts than you had perhaps anticipated ...

PART II

IMPROVING LEARNING AND MAKING EVERYTHING BETTER

CHAPTER 9

THIRTY EXERCISES TO BUILD RAPPORT, ENCOURAGE SPONTANEITY AND GET THEIR CREATIVE JUICES FLOWING

With the thoughts of Part I still ringing in your ears (or your eyes), take a gander at the following activities and see how simple it is to use humour, comedy and having a laugh to fire up your lessons so that everyone benefits.

EXERCISES TO ENGAGE CURIOSITY

No matter how well you know a person, subject or environment, I believe that there is always more you can discover if you've got the confidence and can be bothered. The exercises that follow are simply a few of the techniques that I use to get students curious, build rapport and engage their naughty little noggins.

1. FESS UP

This exercise can take many forms but essentially it is a conduit through which the students can describe in detail incidents, experiences, successes and failures. Get them to jot down on a piece of paper a silly but true confession regarding an experience they have had. Examples may include:

- Falling downstairs.
- Calling their teacher 'mum'.
- Eating cat food by mistake.
- Eating cat food on purpose.
- Eating cat.

They then scrunch up the paper and put the balls into a hat. You, the teacher, can then randomly pick out several confessions and read them aloud. The class is charged with the job of quickly working out who they think wrote the confession. They are allowed three guesses per confession. Once the student has been identified they can, if they choose, discuss the experience and see how many others in the class have had a similar occurrence in their life. The main point is to have fun and allow the students to enjoy the process of questioning, discovery and the development of peer relationships through the medium of curiosity.

> *I always wanted three kids; now that I've got two, I only want one.*
>
> LEE MACK

2. THAT'S YOU THAT IS

This is a hugely enjoyable game that involves imagination and divergent thinking and encourages students to really commit to a thought, feeling or idea.

A person is picked at random and asked to stand at the front of the class or the centre of a circle of students. They are then asked to conjure up in their head a statement such as 'Has a tidy bedroom', 'Gives money to charity' or 'Never washes their hands after a trip to the toilet'. It is crucial that the statement remains unspoken at this point.

Once the person has come up with their statement – let's say it is 'Has worn a verruca sock' – they then go round the room pointing at each of their classmates in turn and confirming or denying with a simple 'yes' or 'no' whether they believe the student has or hasn't worn a verruca sock. The fun comes from playing around with the degrees of yes or no. The leader may choose to say things like 'Definitely', 'Sometimes' or 'Only at the weekend'. The key to being the leader is to keep an open mind and respond intuitively to the people in front of you. After each go, the curiosity of the class cranks up as everyone is dying to know what the statement is. After the volunteer has finished they can reveal what their statement was and perhaps, if they are feeling brave, give some reasons. Of course, make sure the class remembers the rules of comedy that you drew up in Chapter 6 so no one's feelings get hurt.

3. WORDS THAT AREN'T WORDS BUT SHOULD BE WORDS

I love toying with words that aren't words but should be words, as doing so involves two of my favourite things – curiosity and fun. Here the idea is to mess about and make random connections between seemingly disparate thoughts, feelings and words (which, if you think about it, is essentially what comedians do for a living). The basic idea is this: the group is given the task of creating some new words – words that aren't words but they think should be words (the clue really is in the title). And that's it. Much joy can be had from the suggestions given and the reasons why a particular word should be embraced within our everyday lexicon. You may wish to have a class vote for the most popular word or even compile a list or top ten of the best ones, complete with a definition.

Here are a few examples of words that aren't words but should be words which have been generously donated by my encounters with inquisitive, creative and lexically curious school kids.

- Pissibolity – a bit like 'possibility' but funnier. I love this word and it has remained a firm favourite in the Keeling household ever since I first heard it. Not to be confused with 'impissibolity'.
- Coincimental – describing a coincidence that is so unlikely that it seems crazy.
- Arm knuckle – meaning elbow.
- Liarrhoea – a continuous, unstoppable torrent of lies.
- Flufflewaffering – to employ the word 'flufflewaffer' instead of swearing, as in 'I hate you, you … flufflewaffer'.
- Funner – meaning more fun than fun. This one has crept into everyday use by many a teenager and I am hearing it at least 47 times a week now. What could be less funner?
- Imbollockable – meaning impervious to criticism. Suggested to me by an excitable Year 10 boy and thus

proving his point, as I was laughing too much to tell him off for swearing.

4. LAST FINGER STANDING

This is a really useful game for getting the curiosity juices flowing and for the class to find out a little more about one another. If possible, the class should stand in a circle with each student holding up all ten fingers. One person at a time then asks a personal question that is designed to elicit a 'yes' or 'no' answer. If a student can't answer 'yes' to a question, they lose a finger (not literally, it's not that sort of game). The person with the last finger standing is the winner. The person with two fingers up gets detention.

EXERCISES TO GET THEM MESSING ABOUT AND LEARNING TO FAIL

Next up are a selection of exercises designed to get them thinking, playing and cocking up left, right and centre.

5. ALIEN; COW; TIGER

This is a great warm-up game and energiser that aims to get those taking part in sync with each other and reinforces the point that mistakes can and should be fun. Everyone taking part stands up (preferably in a circle or where they are able to see one another) and has to pick one of the following three characters:

- Alien – to make it clear you are an alien you must place your index fingers on either side of your head as if they were antennae and say 'Na noo na noo' or 'Phone home', like ET. Or maybe something similarly indicative but originating after the 1980s.

- Cow – to become a cow you must bend forwards and make a big, loud, mooing sound. Come on, we've all done it.
- Tiger – to channel your inner tiger you must place your hands in front of you like claws and then roar at the top of your lungs. (When the students do this you will be surprised how theatrical most of their tigers look!)

On the count of three everyone must pick a character pose to strike. The object of the game is for everyone to strike the same character at the same time. This is very unlikely to happen first go but a lot of fun will be had in the process.

6. GO COMPARE

Students are split into pairs and are given a scenario (e.g. a runaway train). They must then argue for 30 seconds why the other person of the two would be the one best equipped to deal with the situation.

Below is a list of other scenarios you may wish to consider:

i Camping holiday in Clacton.

ii Running their own business.

iii Trapped in a cave.

iv You are an Olympic high-board diver.

v You are a monster.

vi You are a supermodel.

The activity promotes quick, divergent thinking as well as imagination and perseverance.

7. FAST FINGER CHIT-CHAT

Students should be split into pairs and then labelled A and B. A must then ask B a series of questions on any topic (or a specific topic if you wish). When a question has been asked, person A must then hold up a certain number of fingers. Person B must then answer the question using the number of words indicated by the number of fingers being displayed (i.e. three fingers = three words). For instance:

> *Person A: Who do you love? (Person A then holds up three fingers)*
>
> *Person B: I love you.*

Much mischief can be made during this game by messing about with the number of fingers shown. It once again challenges the students to think deeply, be specific and cogitate on their answers before giving them. This technique can also be utilised by the teacher for class discussions or as a way of eliciting answers or feedback.

8. DEFINITE DEFINITIONS

I say 'potato', my daughter says 'chips'. I say 'tomato', my daughter says 'ketchup'. My daughter and I may share the same language but that doesn't mean that what I think a word is all about is the same as what she thinks. The same could be said of you and me. Take the word 'INSET'. I hear: an opportunity to try and make a difference to a large group of practising teachers in a fun way and earn a bob or two in the process. You hear: one of only two or three occasions a year when I can actually get to finish the *Guardian*'s crossword. Same word. Different meanings. This exercise plays with this fact and allows you to learn a great deal about your students as people as well as lexicographers.

Simply write a word on the board such as 'individual' or 'family' or 'defunct' (lovely word, defunct) and then ask everyone to write down what their definition of that word is. You may be surprised to find out that some students can't define what seems like an everyday word or that there may be vastly differing ideas across a single group. This exercise focuses our thinking and reveals how we use words constantly without really thinking about or agreeing on their meaning.

(True story: the word 'individual' recently came up at a conference I was at attending for teachers on Philosophy for Children. We had an hour to philosophise about the definition of the word as well as the nature and merits of individuality as a concept. After an hour, we still couldn't decide what the word actually meant but we had all agreed that the car park was inadequate, the biscuits at breaktime were below par and if it's quiche for lunch then somebody is going to get hurt.)

HUMOUR ACTIVITIES

These exercises can be used for shamelessly playing for laughs – with all the benefits that brings.

9. BLANKETY BLANK

This is a fantastic way to get the students' imaginations firing, as well as creating a quiz show feel next time the group has to do a test. In true BBC family viewing in the 1980s style, the teacher reads out a statement such as:

> *School dinners are getting worse. In fact, they are so bad that last week instead of custard I was served two dollops of* ***blank****.*

The students' task, against the clock (call it 15 seconds) is to come up with and jot down a relevant answer that fits in and replaces the *blank*. The winner is the person who has written down the exact answer that the teacher has on his or her piece of paper. So, for instance, the answer for the question above could have been: gruel, sick or Polyfilla.

The great thing about this exercise is that it can be as ridiculous or as subject specific as you like. For example, you could set questions like this:

> *I'm not saying Macbeth was weak, but without his wife by his side he would never have* ***blank*** *or* ***blank****.*
>
> *Dovetail joints are so handy you can't build a* ***blank*** *without them.*
>
> *Your metatarsal bone is connected to your* ***blank****.*
>
> *To make a baby you can't have* ***blank****.*

This game leaves a lot of room for fun and frivolity and there will be plenty of joy from some of the more diverse answers as it gives students the freedom to run wild within their own heads. Which would you rather, a sea of animated faces all laughing together or a sea of faces staring back at you with an expression that's just blank?

10. COMEDY CORNERS

This activity is designed for the students to play with the knowledge they have gained during the lesson. Each corner of the room becomes a designated area of review. You may wish to label them 'Props', 'Song', 'Joke' and 'Story'. You then split the class into four groups and assign each group a corner of the room. They then have five minutes to come up with a short, punchy review of the lesson utilising the title of the corner. You could also give the corners names such as 'Dance', 'Poem', 'Tableau', 'Picture', 'Model', 'Mime' or just make up your own, as long as the students are given permission to run free and get as much as they can remember about the lesson into their review.

11. TALES OF MEMORY AND IMAGINATION

This technique is so simple, yet so effective, and the most rewarding aspect is that it never fails. Write the numbers 1 to 10 on the board and then ask the class to shout out random objects. When you have your ten objects ask the class to split into pairs. The objective is to tell a story incorporating all ten objects in order. Like all good stories, it must begin with 'Once upon a time ...' and end with the line 'The end'. The only other rule is that the story must be as exaggerated, preposterous, colourful and imaginative as possible. You will be surprised how quickly everyone can remember the ten objects in order and with very little effort other than having a laugh. It is then possible to take this technique to the next level and give them ten subject-specific facts or points with which they must concoct an outlandish story.

12. DID YOU HEAR THE ONE ABOUT ...?

Here is a game that creates the perfect opportunity for the students to discover and identify their 'good humour ingredients' (according to Stephanie Davies' *Laughology* – see Chapter 2). The students split themselves into pairs and are then instructed to tell each other a quick, funny story. While one is creasing up at their own particularly hilarious tale of a misunderstanding at the last school disco, the other student's job is to watch their partner like a hawk, absorbing everything they are doing with their face, voice and body. Does the pitch or intonation change? What words are they using? Are they gesticulating? Do they talk faster? What happens to their eyes? And so on. Once we know how to identify 'good humour ingredients', we will know how to replicate them or seek them out in others. You can then take this activity to the next level by asking the students to repeat their story but this time subtly crowbarring in, for comic effect, some of the key content of the lesson.

IMPROV GAMES

Next up are four of my favourite improvisation games. These are guaranteed to get students thinking fast, making decisions, working as a team, developing bravery and firing on however many cylinders they have.[1]

13. THREE-HEADED EXPERT

This is a wonderful way to finish off a session but can also be used to great effect at any point when you feel review would be beneficial. You will require three volunteers (or three students you don't like – same thing). They are to stand at the front of the class and henceforth shall be collectively known as the 'Three-Headed Expert'. That's right, you heard. One body. Three heads. This is where you can have great fun spouting forth about just how clever this expert is. You may wish to inform everyone that this particular authority knows more than anyone else who has ever lived, that they have travelled the globe extensively and really, really been there, done that and not only bought the T-shirt but designed it, manufactured it and Argos-ed it. Oh yes, they know a thing or two ...

Once the set-up is complete you can then inform the inquisitive throng before you that it is now their responsibility to come up with topics to question said expert about. It is a good idea at this point to reassure the specialist that they cannot get anything wrong. After all, they are an expert and have all the answers. You can then take these topics and craft some pointed questions for them to

1 I've met some with seven and some with barely one, no matter what you do to try and rev them up a bit.

answer. You may wish to ask a couple of generic questions first, just to get the Three-Headed Expert warmed up.

When a question has been posed, the expert must answer with one word per head in order of left to right. It is up to you, the facilitator, to decide when you think you have received the desired answer. Once a few general questions have been asked, you can then encourage the students to ask more lesson-specific questions.

This exercise just goes to prove that the students are capable of educating one another. They just need time, space and permission to do it. This game never fails to create laughter and some genuinely insightful, illuminating and cheeky answers.

14. SENTUS INTERRUPTUS

This can be played with the whole class at once or preferably with three students out at the front (find three more you don't like). The idea of the game is this: the class picks a subject that the three volunteers must discuss – for instance, 'The weather'. You, as the facilitator, must decide whose turn it is to talk by pointing at an individual. The rules are that as soon as you have pointed, the person who was talking must finish speaking immediately and the next person must continue speaking where the other left off. An example might go something like this:

> *Person A: The weather will be mainly dry with outbreaks of rain that will continue until morning ...*
>
> *Person B: ... has broken, like the first morning, blackbird has spoken like the first bird ...*
>
> *Person C: ... my first bird was called Julie, but enough of that, here's Johnny with the sport!*

You get the idea. The beauty of this game is that it encourages listening, communication, quick wit and concentration as well as the ability to wax lyrical on any given subject. It tends to work better, and is easier, if the subject is just a starting point from which they can go off in any direction (like the example on page 99). But if you really want to challenge the group, and think they are up for the quest, you may want to keep the whole exchange focused purely on the topic given.

The more confident the group, the quicker the interactions can be between players. You may even wish to let other members of the class become facilitators. The power is in your hands.

15. FUZZY DUCK

In my experience, this game is normally played in the pub after a few pints, but it works just as well sober as a fast lesson-livener. Arrange the group in a circle. Pick someone to start the game by saying 'fuzzy duck', which is then repeated in turn, clockwise around the circle. If someone wants to change the direction they can say 'Does he?' When this happens you then go round in an anticlockwise direction, but this time saying 'ducky fuzz' and so on and so forth. This is a very funny and energetic way to start or break up a session and you can imagine that quite frequently students can get their 'mucking furds in a wuddle'. Guaranteed to get them howling with laughter.

16. EYES SCREAM

This is a classic warm-up and a quick way to get a group working in sync with each other. The group stands in a circle and looks down at the ground. On the count of three everyone looks up at once, looking either to the left, to the right or straight ahead across the circle. If, as they look up, a student makes eye contact with another student then they both must scream and leave the circle. The game continues until everybody is out or the head teacher enters the room to find out why there is quite so much shrieking coming from your RE lesson.

ACTIVITIES TO GET 'EM THINKING, WONDERING, LAUGHING AND LEARNING

A collection of great exercises taken from the weird and wacky world of stand-up and beyond.

17. THAT'S SO RANDOM!

This exercise is simple and easy to set up. You and your class need to find between five and ten random objects around the classroom or school. These can be anything you can get your hands on. The objects are then distributed to small groups or individuals who are given between three and five minutes to link the random object to the subject matter. The teams or individuals then present their object and links back to the class. You could also put the object in the centre of a comedy-gram to see how much fun can be extracted from it.

18. SIX DEGREES OF PREPARATION[2]

Supposedly, in this weird but wondrous world, we are only six people away from anybody, and not just Kevin Bacon. You know somebody who knows somebody who knows somebody who knows somebody who knows somebody who knows Barack Obama or Miss Piggy or Noel Edmonds' cleaning lady. Mind you, with the power of the internet, and how small that makes the world, this could be considerably fewer and you could be closer to Noel Edmonds' domestic arrangements than you think. However, for the sake of this exercise, I shall stick with the number six. A question that is often asked by students is, 'Why are we doing this? No really, sir, what's the point?' Now, rather than the normal 'Coz it's in the exam', 'Coz I say so', 'Coz how else will you ever know how to prune a raspberry bush?' (true story), all you do is take the subject in question and ask your students to come up with six steps that link them to it.

All you do is take the subject in question and ask your students to come up with six ways they can link themselves to it. (It doesn't matter how tenuous the link is as long as it connects to the subject in some way.)

For example, for the Great Fire of London the six links could be:

i I keep a diary. (Samuel Pepys famously wrote about the fire in his diary, which is one of the reasons we now know what happened.)

ii My birthday is on 2 September (when the fire started).

iii 'Firestarter' is a brilliant dance track by The Prodigy.

2 You see what I did there?!

iv My favourite bakery is Greggs (the fire started in a bakery owned by Thomas Farriner).

v I have visited St Paul's Cathedral. (One of the thousands of buildings burned down during the fire.)

vi My favourite bird is a wren. (Sir Christopher Wren designed a monument to remember the Great Fire, which still stands to this day.)

Apart from developing great lateral thinking skills, it also helps to make the learning real and relevant.

19. AGREE/DISAGREE

This is a wonderful opportunity to get the students talking about a subject and debating the facts surrounding it. All you need to prepare are four signs positioned around the room that read 'Agree', 'Disagree', 'Strongly agree' and 'Strongly disagree' and some prepared statements about the subject matter you are studying. These can be true statements, beliefs, non-truths, controversial assertions, made-up rubbish – you decide. You read them out and ask the students to go and stand by the sign that best represents their opinion on the statement that has just been read out. In their groups they then have to come up with a reason why they feel the way they do and be able to put their point across to the class. The next step is to open it up into a debate with the other three groups. Some people may feel indifferent, in which case they should stand in the middle of the room and wait to be convinced by the others. Encourage them also to go against what they are thinking and to stand next to the sign that is the complete opposite to what they believe and see if they can still put together a strong and coherent argument.

20. OBSERVATIONAL LOVELINESS

This Is a really nice exercise to help the students feel good and for them to observe the good in others. While it is not laugh-out-loud hilarious, never underestimate how funny it is watching teenage boys attempt to give each other a compliment. First, put together a list of classmates, perhaps on a spreadsheet. Each class member is given a copy of the spreadsheet and asked to write just one thing next to everyone's name that they think is a nice quality about that person. This can be anything from they are really clever at spelling to they are kind to others in the class. The teacher then collates all the statements and each child eventually receives a hard copy of all the things that are lovely about them. Confidence and knowing your strengths is empowering and, in order to be fully open and playful, we need to feel more confident and good about ourselves. This is a completely anonymous exercise so no one need feel embarrassed about what is written by them or by others.

21. WHAT THE FAQ?

A great title and one which will come as a surprise to many of your congregation and so should be used with care (you know your audience better than I do). The basic premise is to pair up your students and ask them to have a conversation that can consist only of questions. I (Person 1) tried out this exercise on my 11-year-old daughter (Person 2) and this is what I got:

Person 1: Where have you been?

Person 2: What?

Person 1: Can you hear me?

Person 2: Sorry?

Person 1: Am I talking to myself?

Person 2: Come again?

Person 1: Have I not made myself clear?

Person 2: About what?

Person 1: What have I just said?

Person 2: When?

Person 1: Do you want me to get your mother?

Person 2: Why would I want you to do that?

Person 1: Do you not understand what I am trying to say?

Person 2: What are you trying to say?

Person 1: I can't remember!

Aahh, how quickly they grow up and make you feel like the child!

The allure of this one is that it requires a lot of thinking because we are used to answering questions but not always asking them. It helps to develop quick thinking, concision in language and it never fails to take the participants on some very interesting journeys. You may wish to make it more competitive and introduce rules such as time limits or hesitations or simply frame the conversation by setting it in a particular place or during an event. The choice is yours. Just have a laugh with it.

22. I DID IT FIVE WAYS

This little lovely is designed to get the students' imaginations firing off in all directions. Simply pose a challenge and then they have to come up with five ways in which they would rise to that challenge. For example, name five ways you would:

- Make a giraffe cry.

- Hide a car.
- Upset your auntie.
- Eat a chocolate bar.
- Confuse an alien.
- Spend a tenner.
- Convince a stranger that you're actually very successful – no, really ... (welcome to my world).

Answers can be compiled and awards, treats or doctor's notes can be given for the funniest, weirdest, simplest, scariest and so on.

23. WOULD YOU RATHER?

This exercise builds on the one above. A double-headed question is put to the class and the only rule is that they have to pick one of the questions. Here are some I prepared earlier. Would you rather ...

Eat a bowl of sprouts every day for a year?

Or

Give yourself three paper cuts every day for a year?

Run a mile as fast as you can?

Or

Hang upside down for ten minutes?

Have a massive right leg?

Or

Be eight stone overweight?

Live on your own forever?

Or

Live with three others who are all annoying?

The fun comes from the diverse reasons and arguments that are given. Trust me, they will be weird, wonderful and, in some cases, incredibly persuasive.

24. WONDROUS WONDERINGS

These are phantasmagorical questions of frolicsome fancy designed to promote deep thinking and reflection and will, if allowed, elicit much fun and frivolity. Here are ten of my favourites:

i Which would be best: making all your decisions with your head or with your heart?

ii If your insides were outside, would you be healthier?

iii Which finger is best?

iv If your life up to now had been one long interview, would you get the job?

v If spiders wore silly spectacles and dungarees, would you still be scared?

vi If you could enjoy food only through touch, what foods would you pick?

vii If you could think yourself fit, how fit would you be?

viii If every experience was from a catalogue, which ones would be returns, which would you keep and which ones are you still paying for now?

ix What is your kryptonite?

x Have you already had the best present ever?

25. WORD UP

The simple premise behind this activity is for students to take responsibility for collecting six key words from a session and then, at the end, constructing a catchy sound bite. These can then be collected together to form a record of key themes/ideas/facts from the lesson. You can, of course, experiment with the number of words to be collected and what form you wish the record to take, such as a jingle, poem, quote, catchphrase and so on. You may also flag up at the beginning that you will be uttering six very important words during the session which you have concealed in a golden envelope and there will be a prize for anyone who gets all six right. There's nothing like creating some competitive edge to get the attention of the learners completely focused.

26. DEVIL'S AVOCADO

I love this game mainly because I love to argue the toss. It's my inner teenager. Devil's avocado is geared towards testing your nerve and quick wit, not to mention your reasoning skills. An opinion is put forward during a lesson and then someone is picked to take on the role of devil's avocado. Their job is to simply present a solid and well thought out counter-argument. The winner is the person whose argument is the most convincing. Their reward is an avocado.

Lots of fun can be had just trying to come up with as many ways to go against the original idea as possible. The more outlandish it is, the funnier it is. You will also find that the general debate is both informative and surprising.

Feel free to use some of the examples below as a starting point to argue against:

- Everyone should go to school.
- We should never steal.
- What goes up must come down.
- We should always be nice to everyone.
- It is always better to be an individual.
- Britain has got talent.
- As you get older you get wiser.
- Football is the best sport ever.
- We are all born equal.
- Fast food is bad for you.

27. AND THEN WHAT HAPPENED?

This game works best in pairs or groups of four. The group decides on an opening statement such as:

> *I was on my way back to Claire's Accessories ... [It's a long story]*

One of the group then volunteers to go first and utters the opening sentence. The group then responds to this statement, and to all subsequent ones, with the phrase:

> *And then what happened?*

The volunteer's job is to keep coming up with new, bigger and bolder statements until the time limit is up. I suggest that for the first go you set a limit of a minute (it will seem longer than you think!). The game is a superb test of the students' ability to keep building one idea after another and to see how far they can plumb the deep recesses of their minds to consistently come up with a narrative. A lot of joy can be had by all, watching and waiting to see where the story goes. Of course, the opening sentence can be linked to your lesson in a subject-specific way if you like.

28. THINK/KNOW/NEVER FORGET

This exercise is an effective way to 'capture' learner progress throughout the lesson. At the beginning, state the topic or theme of the lesson and give the students a couple of minutes to record *what they think they know* about it already. Then, make sure that throughout the lesson the students record *what they now know* thanks to the lesson they are experiencing. Finally, at the end, spend a couple of minutes asking the students to record *what they will never forget*. (There must always be one thing a lesson that the students will never forget and, sometimes, you won't be surprised to find out, it's got nothing to do with the lesson.) This is a simple and fun way to manage students' expectations, empower them and show them how much learning can take place in one lesson.

29. YOU'RE HAVING A LAUGH

Sometimes you don't even need to create anything funny for people to have a laugh – it's just a question of giving them permission to let it all hang out just a little bit more. This task, like many of the others in this book, is effectively effortless and requires practically no set-up. All you need to do is create a clear signal, such as when you bang the desk, ring a bell, say a codeword or something similar. Whenever this signal is enacted, the class must laugh. And they laugh until they hear the signal again. Much amusement can be had experimenting with how we laugh, how loud a noise we make, the faces we pull, who we are laughing with and the like. Without a shadow of a doubt, the energy in the room will increase and all the good chemicals mentioned in Chapter 4 will be released. They say that laughter is good for the soul. It's also a good way to break up a lesson.

30. SKETCH CLUB

With ten minutes to go to the end of the lesson, the class is split into groups of six. They are then set the task of coming up with a 60-second sketch that involves all six of them, the main aim of which is to lampoon the lesson. And when I say lampoon, like a two-bit actor in a Mexican soap opera, I'm talking exaggeration, exaggeration, exaggeration. They should use key words, main themes, unexpected events that happened during the lesson, your traits and tics (go on, you can take it – it's for a good cause), objects and kit that were employed – anything and everything is game as long as they adhere to the humour rules laid out in Chapter 6. You'll be amazed what is remembered, how much is remembered and how much attention the learners pay during the lesson knowing this exercise will be coming up.

For over 200 more exercises like the 30 provided here, to delight, challenge and engage students and teachers alike, look no further than *Rocket Up Your Class!* and *Invisible Teaching*. But then I would say that ...

CHAPTER 10

GAGGING FOR MORE?

No one ever died from laughter.

MAX BEERBHOM

TWENTY REASONS TO USE LAUGHTER IN YOUR LESSONS

Hopefully this book, if it has done anything, has whetted your appetite and left you gagging for more fun and frivolity in your classroom. But for those of you who have managed to get this far, but are still not convinced that there is any real fun to be had in a classroom, here are 20 of the best reasons to bring laughter to work with you:

1 Encourages enthusiasm.

2 Creates confidence for trying new things.

3 Develops a richer understanding of the subject matter.

4 Brings passion to a subject that could otherwise be dry.

5 Improves the immune system, increasing attendance – yours and theirs.

6 Expands communication skills.

7 Teaches resilience.

8 Enhances creativity.

9 Makes you, the teacher, more engaging and cool (honest!).

10 Keeps your learners wide awake with increased oxygen to the brain for alertness and concentration.

11 Creates a feel-good environment to work in.

12 Motivates and inspires others to bring more laughter into their lives and classrooms.

13 Makes you and your learners happier.

14 Reduces conflict between classmates and between learners and the teacher.

15 Increases self-esteem.

16 Creates a learning environment that is open to new ideas.

17 Brings optimism into learning.

18 Creates rapport between teachers and learners.

19 Ensures that whatever you're doing doesn't feel like work.

20 Improves everyone's capacity to retain and remember the content of a lesson.

TWENTY OBJECTS FOR YOUR COMEDY KITBAG

I have always found that a great way to brighten up a lesson is to introduce some fun objects into the proceedings – you can quite literally use anything. However, it is always a good idea to have a 'comedy kitbag' to hand that you can deploy at any time the need arises. Here are some examples of what you might want to have in yours:

1 Fun stickers – everyone loves a sticker, even adults. Go and plant one on the head today!
2 Comedy pen or pencil.
3 Sponge hammer – always useful to bash out an answer from those students who are too fond of the 'I dunno' response.
4 Wig(s) – if you or the students are to take on a different character.
5 Comedy specs – to give what you are about to say more kudos and weight.
6 White lab coat – not just for scientists and mad doctors.
7 Fog horn – for attention and to start or stop an exercise.
8 Buzzer or ding bell – for quizzes.
9 Sweets – allergies should always be thought about before offering any sweets or food (and they are not just for you to nibble on during break).
10 Music player – to be used as a reward or to bring the energy up or calm it down.
11 Playing cards – for magic tricks, status exercises, numbering systems, group work and so on.
12 Rubber brain – always good to review how clever we are or for emphasising an academically important point.
13 Glove puppet – when you don't want to talk any more.

14 Juggling balls – to be used as another way of conducting a hands-free debate. Simply chuck a ball at an unsuspecting student and when they catch it they have to make a verbal contribution.

15 Pointy stick and/or laser pen – to point things out and add massive memorable emphasis to anything it is directed at.

16 Box of awe and wonder – to foster curiosity and create excitement around any topic.

17 A coin – for heads and tails.

18 Whoopee cushion – what young (or old) person doesn't find whoopee cushions amusing?

19 Selection of great TV and movie tunes – these will add atmosphere, fun and gravitas to any exercise.

20 A cape – you know you want to!

TEN GREAT FREE APPS FOR COMIC (AND EDUCATIONAL) EFFECT IN THE CLASSROOM

If you have a smartphone with apps, check out the ten little beauties that follow, which are great for getting students' attention, creating a playful atmosphere and emphasising points throughout a lesson:

1 3D Brain (Cold Spring Harbor Laboratory) – you can literally mess with your own head and see what bit does what.

2. TED (TED Conferences LLC) – this great app is a quick way into a world full of weird, wonderful, funny and engaging talks on a myriad of topics.
3. Magic Tricks Pro (FreshPaper Media LLC) – allows you to build up a repertoire of magic tricks to bamboozle your class and develop audience participation.
4. Johnny Magic Soundboard (Johnny Magic LLC) – allows you to create the feel of a quiz at the touch of a button.
5. The Star Wars App – when your wisdom is ignored, sometimes it's useful to turn to a professional Jedi.
6. Atomic Fart (FAR Apps) – there are loads of these so my advice is try out a few and see which ones are the most realistic and hilarious. C'mon! If it's good enough for the Sumerians ...
7. Fun Sound Effects & Noises (iGreenEarth) – gives you 100 sound effects to pimp up your classroom content in an auditory way.
8. Epic Jokes – Best Jokes Ever (Epic Digital Works LTD) – for those of you who don't relish the thought of writing your own material, here is an app with more jokes than Jimmy Carr.
9. Quipper Quiz (Quipper Ltd) – like having the Eggheads in your back pocket. This is an app that can create instant quizzes on a whole host of topics.
10. X Factor Voiceover Man (FreemantleMedia Ltd) – OK, I know at the top it says 'free' but this one only costs 99p and that is a small price to pay to make every lesson feel like *Britain's Got Talent* or *The X Factor*. As soon as you hear this man's voice, you immediately feel like something monumental is happening – and

you can input your own phrases for more bespoke announcements. Class for your class!

TWENTY REASONS WHY YOUR WORK HERE IS NOT YET DONE

1 *Q. Name the four seasons.*

A. Salt, pepper, mustard and vinegar.

2 *Q. What happens to your body as you age?*

A. When you get old, so do your bowels and you get intercontinental.

3 *Q. Where does the sky start?*

A. When you get the Digibox.

4 *Q. What does benign mean?*

A. Benign is what you will be after you be eight.

5 *Q. Name a major disease associated with cigarettes.*

A. Premature death.

6 *Q. Name one of the early Romans' greatest achievements.*

A. Learning to speak Latin.

7 *Q. To change centimetres to metres you ...?*

A. Take out centi.

8 *Q. What ended in 1896?*

A. 1895.

9 *Q. Where was the American Declaration of Independence signed?*

A. At the bottom.

10 *Q. The first cells were probably ...?*

A. Lonely.

11 *Q. What do we call the classification of living things?*

A. Racism.

12 *Q. Why are there rings on Saturn?*

A. Because God liked it, so he put a ring on it. Saturn was **not** *a single lady.*

13 *Q. Can a man still reproduce with only one testicle?*

A. No, women don't find that attractive.

14 *Q. Imagine that you lived at the same time as Abraham Lincoln. What would you say to him or ask him?*

A. I'd tell him not to go to a play ever.

15 *Q. Miranda can't see anything when she looks down her microscope. Suggest a reason why.*

A. She is blind.

16 *Q. Explain the phrase 'free press'.*

A. When your mum irons your trousers for you.

17 *Q. What is a common treatment for a badly bleeding nose?*

A. Circumcision.

18 *Q. Name six animals that live specifically in the Arctic.*

A. Two polar bears and four seals.

19 *Q. What is the highest frequency noise that a human can register?*

A. Mariah Carey.

20 *Q. How important are elections to a democratic society?*

A. Sex can only happen when a male gets an election.

FINAL THOUGHTS

Before I go I'd like to leave you, as most comedians usually do, with a little story.

Two bulls – one young and full of enthusiasm, the other older and wiser – see a herd of cows. The young bull says, 'Let's charge down the hillside and have our wicked way with a couple of cows!'

To which the old bull replies, 'No, how about we stroll down the hillside and have our wicked way with all of them.'

Like a lot of old bull, there is much truth there. But before you rush off with the wrong end of the stick, and end up on the RSPCA's most-wanted list, let me reassure you that I have thrown many years' worth of experience and practice into the pages of this little book, but that doesn't mean to say you have to throw everything you've read into your first week of lessons. All this is likely to do is to freak everyone out and leave you with a banging headache and an exclusion order.

My best advice is that you take the ideas from this book and ease them into your everyday practice, in order to support, enhance, reinforce and galvanise the great work that you are already responsible for in your classroom. Don't throw out your years of experience and insert mine. Take my ideas, play with them, integrate them and, more importantly, make them yours. All I ask is that you keep in contact and let me know what and how you are implementing *Independent Thinking on Laughter* into your daily educational comings and goings.

So, before I bow out, I would like the cheeky, but never blue, Northern comedian Lee Mack to sum up the real spirit of this book in just one sentence:

> *The idea in life is to mess about until the day you die.*

There you have it. That's philosophy for you. So, now, it only remains for me to say:

> *Ladies and gentlemen, you've been a wonderful audience. My name's Dave Keeling. Thanks for reading and goodnight.*

Email me: david.keeling@independentthinking.co.uk

Follow me on Twitter: @mrappealing

APPENDIX 1

INDEX OF EXERCISES

THIRTY EXERCISES TO BUILD RAPPORT, ENCOURAGE SPONTANEITY AND GET THEIR CREATIVE JUICES FLOWING

APPENDIX 2

LIST OF LISTS

REFERENCES AND FURTHER READING

Brain, M. (2000) How Laughter Works, HowStuffWorks.com (1 April). Available at: http://science.howstuffworks.com/life/laughter.htm.

Branson, R. (2006) *Screw It, Let's Do It: Lessons in Life* (London: Virgin Books/Ebury).

Charlton, B. G. (2006) The Rise of the Boy-Genius: Psychological Neoteny, Science and Modern Life, *Medical Hypotheses* 67(4): 679–681. Available at: http://www.hedweb.com/bgcharlton/ed-boygenius.html.

Curran, A. (2008) *The Little Book of Big Stuff about the Brain: The True Story of Your Amazing Brain* (Carmarthen: Crown House Publishing).

Davies, S. (2013) *Laughology: Improve Your Life with the Science of Laughter* (Carmarthen: Crown House Publishing).

Friedman, T. L. (2013) It's P.Q. and C.Q. as Much as I.Q., *New York Times* (29 January). Available at: http://www.nytimes.com/2013/01/30/opinion/friedman-its-pq-and-cq-as-much-as-iq.html?_r=0.

Gervais, M. and Wilson, D. S. (2005) The Evolutions and Functions of Laughter and Humor: A Synthetic Approach, *Quarterly Review of Biology* 80(4): 395–430.

Jacobi, S. (2005) *Laughing Matters* (London: Arrow Books/Random House).

Johnstone, K. (1989) *Impro: Improvisation and the Theatre* (London: Methuen Drama).

Kay, P. (2004) *Live at the Top of the Tower* [DVD] (London: Universal Pictures UK).

Keeling, D. (2009) *Rocket Up Your Class! 101 High Impact Activities to Start, End and Break Up Lessons* (Carmarthen: Crown House Publishing).

Keeling, D. and Hodgson, D. (2011) *Invisible Teaching: 101 Ways to Create Energy, Openness and Focus in the Classroom* (Carmarthen: Crown House Publishing).

Koestler, A. (1964) *The Act of Creation* (New York: Penguin).

Martin, S. (2008) *Born Standing Up: A Comic's Life* (New York: Pocket Books).

Morreall, J. (1983) *Taking Laughter Seriously* (Albany, NY: State University of New York Press).

Morris, D. (1967) *The Naked Ape: A Zoologist's Study of the Human Animal* (New York: McGraw-Hill).

Ofsted (2019) *The Education Inspection Framework*. Ref: 190015. Available at: https://assets.publishing.service.gov.uk/government/uploads/system/uploads/attachment_data/file/801429/Education_inspection_framework.pdf.

Smith, J. (2017) *The Lazy Teacher's Handbook – New Edition: How Your Students Learn More When You Teach Less* (Carmarthen: Independent Thinking Press).

Vorhaus, J. (1994) *The Comic Toolbox: How to Be Funny Even if You're Not* (Beverly Hills, CA: Silman-James Press).

INDEPENDENT
THINKING ON ...

978-178135337-0

978-178135338-7

978-178135339-4

978-178135340-0

978-178135341-7

978-178135353-0

independent thinking press

www.independentthinkingpress.com

ALSO BY DAVE KEELING

978-184590134-9

978-184590685-6

FEATURING DAVE KEELING

978-190442438-3

independent thinking press

www.independentthinkingpress.com

James Bryan Smith

The Good and Beautiful JOURNAL

An imprint of InterVarsity Press
Downers Grove, Illinois

InterVarsity Press
P.O. Box 1400, Downers Grove, IL 60515-1426
ivpress.com
email@ivpress.com

InterVarsity Press® is a resource publishing division of InterVarsity Christian Fellowship/USA®. For information, visit intervarsity.org.

Cover design and image composite: Cindy Kiple
Interior design: Daniel van Loon
Image: © Yothin Sanchai / EyeEm / Getty Images

ISBN 978-1-5140-0586-6 (print)

Printed in the United States of America ♾

InterVarsity Press is committed to ecological stewardship and to the conservation of natural resources in all our operations. This book was printed using sustainably sourced paper.

P 17 16 15 14 13 12 11 10 9 8 7 6 5 4 3 2 1
Y 37 36 35 34 33 32 31 30 29 28 27 26 25 24 23 22